Praise for *What Grows in Weary Lands*

"We live in an increasingly weary world. So many of us are bone-tired—tired of all the noise, the hurry, the drama, and, at times, even tired of prayer. In our cultural moment of chronic exhaustion, Tish Harrison Warren offers us a spirituality for the weary. A map for the desert. A literary guide to gently companion us through the dark night of the soul. Warren is one of our best living spiritual writers; her ability to blend Christian spirituality and insights from church history with beautifully down-to-earth honesty and raw humor, all while keeping our soul hopeful in God, is a rare gift. It would be impossible to overstate how warmly I recommend this book to all, but especially to the 'weary and heavy laden' of the kingdom."

—John Mark Comer, *New York Times* bestselling author of *Practicing the Way* and *The Ruthless Elimination of Hurry*

"Tish Harrison Warren has written the book we need in this time as believers, as neighbors, and as men and women navigating the modern world."

—Annie F. Downs, *New York Times* bestselling author of *That Sounds Fun*

"I have loved all of Tish Harrison Warren's books, but I may have a new favorite. *What Grows in Weary Lands* is a rich application of ancient monastic wisdom to the burnout tendencies of modern life. You need to read it."

—Justin Whitmel Earley, author of *Habits of the Household* and *The Body Teaches the Soul*

"*What Grows in Weary Lands* is the book I needed to read to refresh my soul and invigorate my faith. Tish Harrison Warren plumbs the wisdom of the Desert Fathers and Mothers, using their struggles with God to speak to our weary and burned-out age. If you are looking for a way of being Christian when you feel like you are at the end of your rope, this is the book for you. Warren is one of the best spiritual writers of our day, and this may be her best work to date."

—Esau McCaulley, PhD, professor at Wheaton College, author of *How Far to the Promised Land*

"What I love about Tish Harrison Warren's writing is her clarity about both desolation and consolation—her honesty and her hope. In this she is much like the Desert Fathers and Mothers, and in this book she connects our spiritual struggles to theirs, and their journey to holiness with ours. Read this book if you have discovered that you do not get through life without going through a desert; read this book to discover that the desert brings a kind of life you cannot find anywhere else."

—Andy Crouch, partner for theology and culture, Praxis; author of *The Life We're Looking For*

"This book is too good simply to be read—it must be conversed with. Warren writes in such a way that often—sometimes more than once on a page—I had to stop and journal or stop and pray. Whatever spiritual season in which a reader approaches this book, there are gifts abundant. Her honesty and hope bring balm to the soul of the hurting and zeal to the heart of the eager."

—Rev. Dr. Amy Peeler, professor at Wheaton College, associate rector at St. Mark's Episcopal Church (Geneva, Ill.), author of *Women and Gender of God*

"This book is like a friend who reminds you who you are and who God is when you're too weary to remember. It's a theology of staying-put—a gospel for those of us in the long middle of faith who are tired not because we've lost our faith, but because we've kept it. I found myself pausing and relishing so many sentences as the truth sank in—just because I can't see growth, doesn't mean it's not happening. On behalf of weary pilgrims I say thank you, Tish!"

—Jon Guerra, devotional music singer-songwriter

"With penetrating insight and disarming honesty, *What Grows in Weary Lands* retrieves and applies the ancient wisdom sorely needed in our distracted and burned-out age. This book is a tall glass of living water for parched, weary lives. It is poised to become a modern spiritual classic and another must-read offering from one of the brightest spiritual writers of our day."

—Rev. Claude Atcho, pastor of Church of the Resurrection (Charlottesville, Va.), author of *Rhythms of Faith* and *Reading Black Books*

"Honest, wise, and persistent in imagination, this is a book to refresh the seasoned spiritual traveler. A beautifully crafted weave of both resilience and wonder."

—Martin Shaw, author of *Liturgies of the Wild*

By Tish Harrison Warren

Advent

Prayer in the Night

Liturgy of the Ordinary

Little Prayers for Ordinary Days

What Grows in Weary Lands

What Grows in Weary Lands

On Christian Resilience

Tish Harrison Warren

CONVERGENT
NEW YORK

Convergent
An imprint of Random House
A division of Penguin Random House LLC
1745 Broadway, New York, NY 10019
convergentbooks.com
penguinrandomhouse.com

LIBRARY OF CONGRESS CATALOGING-IN-PUBLICATION DATA
Names: Harrison Warren, Tish, 1979- author
Title: What grows in weary lands / by Tish Harrison Warren.
Description: First edition. | New York, NY: Convergent, [2026] | Includes bibliographical references. | Identifiers: LCCN 2026004058 (print) | LCCN 2026004059 (ebook) | ISBN 9780593728840 hardcover | ISBN 9780593728857 ebook
Subjects: LCSH: Spiritual life—Christianity | Spiritual formation | Hidden God | Wilderness (Theology) | Perseverance (Theology)
Classification: LCC BV4501.3 .H374 2026 (print) | LCC BV4501.3 (ebook)
LC record available at https://lccn.loc.gov/2026004058
LC ebook record available at https://lccn.loc.gov/2026004059

Printed in the United States of America

1st Printing

First Edition

BOOK TEAM: Production editor: Michelle Daniel • Managing editor: Allison Fox • Production manager: Sarah Feightner • Copy editor: Ethan Campbell • Proofreaders: Michael Burke, Andrea Gordon, Rachel Kirsch, Carrie Krause

Book design by Susan Turner

The authorized representative in the EU for product safety and compliance is Penguin Random House Ireland, Morrison Chambers, 32 Nassau Street, Dublin D02 YH68, Ireland. https://eu-contact.penguin.ie

For Marcia Bosscher,
who knew I was a writer before I did
and taught me about tending the fire.

And for all those whose faithfulness
has made me want to be faithful.

Above all, trust in the *slow* work of God. We are, quite naturally, impatient in everything to reach the end without delay. We should like to skip the intermediate stages. We are impatient of being *on the way* to something *unknown*, something *new*. And yet it is the law of all progress that it is made by passing through some stages of instability—and that may take a very long time.

—Pierre Teilhard de Chardin[1]

Many claim to have been born again, but the evidence for mature Christian discipleship is slim. In our kind of culture anything, even news about God, can be sold if it is packaged freshly; but when it loses its novelty, it goes on the garbage heap. There is a great market for religious experience in our world; there is little enthusiasm for the patient acquisition of virtue, little inclination to sign up for a long apprenticeship in what earlier generations of Christians called holiness.

—Eugene H. Peterson[2]

We know that suffering produces perseverance; perseverance, character; and character, hope.

—Romans 5:3–4 (niv)

CONTENTS

PROLOGUE

Tending the Fire

The fire would not start.

I lit one match after another and held it under the kindling. The match would flame—bright, cheery, growing—and then abruptly wither, giving up its ghost.

My work was in vain. And I was cold.

I had ended up in front of this dark fireplace at a retreat center in the Texas Hill Country because I needed an escape. I'd come feeling profoundly weary. Soul weary. Body weary. Weary of being weary. My life back home was still busy and productive. I wrote weekly for *The New York Times*, which was a dream job in many ways. I was also working on a book, serving a church, and raising three kids who generally got fed each day. I was, in a broad sense, okay. But I was running on sheer adrenaline nearly all the time, and I knew that could not last. I was spent.

I hoped to hide out for a few days amid these craggy hills to pray and to work. Here, hawks glided over slate-colored cliffs along the slow Frio River. Here, maybe I'd have a chance to hear something my soul was trying to say. Maybe it was quiet enough to notice the still, small voice of God, and to find inspiration, transcendence, a handhold.

It was freezing outside, so I'd decided to light a fire in the cavernous fireplace in the empty gathering space at the retreat center. It was not going well.

I kept trying, piling up kindling, rearranging logs. But every match burned out. I grew frustrated. I cursed at the matchsticks. I sighed heavily. In college, my friend Jen had nicknamed me "the Firestarter" after I worked wonders on an unusually wet camping trip. I thought I was good at this. I used to be good at this. But the logs were not catching. Nothing was alight.

There was enough fire imagery in my early Christian formation to alarm a park ranger. In my high school youth group, we sang a song every week asking God to "light the fire in my weary soul." Our church camp theme one year was "Light the Fire." In college, I sometimes attended a campus ministry called "Forest Fire" (a clever pun, because I went to Wake Forest University—get it?).

I never thought much about what, specifically, it looked like to be "on fire" for Jesus, but it seemed to be the goal of Christian discipleship. I suppose I wanted a certain emotional experience. I wanted to *feel* full of faith, of zeal, of certainty, of strength. I wanted to have a direct experience of God's constant presence. This desire is not bad.

But what about the times when the fire will not start?

On the three-hour drive from my home to the retreat center, I had rung up my friend Marcia. She was my first editor, and I still talk with her when things feel too heavy or too hard. I told her I felt burned out. I told her I didn't know how to keep going in my life, work, or faith. I told her God felt distant, and any "muse" in my writing was, likewise, nowhere to be found.

Marcia is wise and patient with me. She said that spiritual growth and artmaking alike are usually not found in a sudden insight, like a burst of a flame, but in "the steady laying on of the logs"—in the long, sometimes monotonous tending of a fire—a fire that sputters, dwindles, burns out, and then, at times unexpectedly, flickers back to life.

As I sat at the retreat center, burning through matchsticks, I thought about Marcia's words. I'd take a break from my efforts and stare into the dark fireplace, praying about my life, my sense of lostness and desolation. I'd journal and read a Psalm, and then go back to the kindling again. Still, nothing was happening. Time seemed to stretch endlessly into the frigid night.

I just kept going, adding to my log pile, striking matches, rearranging tinder. Then suddenly, one more try, one more match, and the flame caught and blazed to life. Within minutes, the fire I'd hoped for was warming my hands, the heat flushing my cheeks, the flames brilliant and cheerful.

And the metaphor was not lost on me. All that kindling—all those logs and twigs and shreds of newspaper that had piled up over empty hours—fed the flame. All that time, it had felt like nothing was happening. But every bit of kindling I piled up in frustration fed the fire before me.

The fire burned for hours. I sat by it late into the night, gazing at it quietly. Those flickering flames whispered hope. They told me that this time in my life—a season that seemed as if nothing was alight—was, if I could trust it, a time of tending that, in the hands of God, had meaning and purpose. I cannot force fire. I cannot make it spark to life on my timeline, through my skill, or by my willpower. It's a mystery how it comes at all.

But I can wait. I can keep going. The practices of our faith, acts of perseverance and trust that may feel futile, are at last the fragile kindling set ablaze by the Spirit, at just the right time. In the end, it all feeds the flame. In the end, nothing will be wasted.

What Grows in Weary Lands

1

Discovery in the Desert

lost and found in a weary land

I.

Though we experience this differently, all of us hit points in our lives where we're out of steam, where we can't get traction, where we feel lifeless or tired, disoriented and unsure of ourselves. Things seem hard, maybe harder than we think they should be.

Paul wrote to the early church in Galatia urging them to "not become weary in doing good, for at the proper time we will reap a harvest if we do not give up."[1] But he would not have needed to issue this reminder if the course of life—even a life of faith—did not often make us weary. If the Christian life were meant to feel like a perpetual rock concert or an ecstatic mystical journey, if it was not difficult to pray or believe or obey God, the apostle would not have had to encourage us to keep going, to not give up. Instead, he implies that doing good—that staying true to the commitments of our lives—comes with a cost.

In the past few years, I found myself in something akin to a spiritual drought or a desert, yearning for rain, for renewal. I did not know how to name what I was experiencing. It was not a time of tragedy or deepest suffering, but neither was I flourishing. To call it a midlife crisis feels too dismissive and cliché. There was no plastic surgery or Botox. I didn't run off with some charming stranger I'd met in a hot yoga class or "find myself" in some exotic locale. This was a quiet crisis, as inarticulable as it was unignorable. And it touched nearly every realm of my life.

I had written for *The New York Times* every week for two years. I'd published tens of thousands of words about the value of faith in public discourse and private life. And I had believed them, every word. But my actual faith—my connection to God in a typical day—felt wavering. God began to seem less like a kind, present friend and more like a corpse on a table that we, like medical examiners, analyzed and debated in the comment sections of my articles. Less like a being of overwhelming beauty, the Maker of heaven and earth, and more of a sociological artifact used to track American voting blocs.

Prayer grew halting and frustrating. I would sit to pray, but it felt as though the line had gone dead. I did not feel a sense of God's nearness. I didn't feel much of anything at all. And I'd begin to think, *Is anyone there? Am I fooling myself? Is this a waste of my time?*

At work, I met deadlines. I got positive feedback. But I had lost much of the initial joy I'd had when I first became a writer. Once words flowed from me, feeling electric, urgent, and at times ecstatic. Now my mind meandered and froze. I'd write a sentence and delete it. I'd stare at the empty page. Then came a heaviness in my limbs, a sighing in the soul. Sometimes I'd get up from my desk, lower myself onto the floor, and weakly moan, thinking about how my once beloved work now felt like pushing a boulder up a hill—punishing and pointless. Like Sisyphus, if he were under deadline. I'd stare at the ceiling and wonder, *Am I just being lazy? Am I a fraud? Is it time to give up?*

It seemed I was always worrying over something or other. The online critics, whose voices echoed in my head like some kind of demon parrot who only knew insults. Or the headlines that blared on my news feed. Or the feuding state of the American church. Or my slowing metabolism and sudden appearance of gray hair, which my youngest daughter had kindly begun referring to as my "tinsel."

I wasn't sure anymore who I was, where I was in life, or how to keep going. I was disoriented.

At the same time, I felt overwhelmingly and unavoidably busy, sandwiched between kids—a preschooler, a tween, and a teen—

and an aging mother who, for over a decade, had drifted slowly into the fog of Alzheimer's. They needed me, all in vastly different ways. My husband needed me. Friends needed me. The dog needed me. The church needed me. The chores and bills needed me. I, on the other hand, wanted to crawl into a cave and hide from it all for a few weeks or years or decades.

I had grown weary. But I wasn't sure what to do next.

In the midst of this season, on one ordinary day, my husband Jonathan and I had been low-key squabbling on and off for hours, both feeling crabby. I was tired after a bad night of sleep. Writing that day had felt like a failure, and I'd gotten a discouraging comment from a colleague. I had not used my time well and felt wired and addled from being plugged in to distant sorrows and debates online all day. And as the sun set, my daughter and I got in an argument—I don't even recall about what.

And I'd had it. The walls were closing in on me. I grabbed the car keys, slammed the door, and sped down the street. But where was I to go? I had no idea. So I just drove around, the anger in my chest melting into hot tears until I couldn't see the road anymore. I pulled into an empty Barnes & Noble parking lot, turned off the engine, and wept as I wailed six words that I've since yelled at God a hundred more times: "I don't know what to do!"

Silence. There was no voice speaking back, no flash of insight or clarity, no "heart strangely warmed."[2] After a long while, my tears slowed, my breathing steadied, and I drove back home.

In some ways, it's a stupid story to share—so common it doesn't feel worth writing about. The headline would never go viral: "Middle-Aged White Lady Drives to Strip Center Parking Lot, Cries."

What would have made it worth telling is if I'd kept driving, escaped to Mexico, had an epic adventure, and discovered some zingy new spirituality. Or if I'd walked into the Barnes & Noble, stole something, and slowly broken bad into a life of crime. Or if I'd stopped somewhere to drown my sorrows, bumped into an old flame, and we both realized that everything in the last twenty years had led us to this very moment, together at last. All of that would make good fodder for a memoir. I could spin it all to sound courageous, deep, and original. I would tell how I invented my own path and learned to embrace radical self-love. It would be romantic, passionate, and possibly lucrative.

Instead, I just drove home, with my face all puffy, to put the kids to bed, reconcile with my daughter and husband, and get some sleep. And in our moment in history, such an ending to this small story does not seem brave or profound or worthwhile. Because of this, we end up not telling the stories of these weary yet undramatic seasons—unless those stories end in a total dismantling and reinvention of our lives.

It is vulnerable to talk about long seasons of unfulfillment and of spiritual, creative, and emotional dryness. We can feel as if we are simply being whiny or wimpy. We can tell ourselves we just need to get over it, stop moaning, cheer up. We can also fear that if something feels off or unsatisfying about our life, we must be doing it wrong. We must have made poor choices or forsaken the blissful path we were made for.

But because we don't sit with these stories, we lack the resources to understand what is happening to us when these wearying seasons inevitably come. We miss what these times are meant to do in us, what they shift and grow within us, what they call forth from us, and where God may be in the midst of them. We miss the gifts they offer, gifts we desperately need if we are to flourish.

II.

Several years before this exhausted season, a publisher contacted me out of the blue and suggested I write a book on burnout. I decided not to. *What do I know about burnout?* I thought. I write on spiritual formation and theology, not business management techniques.

Burnout seemed like the property of occupational psychologists, HR seminars, and corporate executives who worked ninety-hour weeks. It seemed like a buzzword in articles on "life hacks" and books about time management. Besides, I thought, it doesn't take a whole book to say, "Practice a Sabbath day. See your loved ones. Get more sleep."

Jump ahead a few years, and here I was, even as I kept a Sabbath day each week, spent time with my loved ones, and (more or less) got sleep, still feeling lost and weary. And it started to seem that all around me, other people felt the same.

During the Covid years, and now in the years since, burnout was suddenly everywhere. Major outlets like the *Times* and *The Atlantic* began reporting on rising levels of parental burnout, caretaker burnout, ministry burnout, social media burnout, professional burnout, political burnout, and marital burnout.[3] Book titles addressing burnout soared to bestsellerdom. The journalist Ezra Klein called burnout "an omnipresent diagnosis of modernity."[4] It seems as though a pall of collective exhaustion and despondency has settled over our society.

Other words began to circulate as we tried to understand this general sense of fatigue and stress. In 2021, Adam Grant wrote in the *Times* about a phenomenon that he says is neither burnout nor depression. He called it "languishing." He described it as feeling "somewhat joyless and aimless" with "a sense of stagnation and emptiness . . . as if you're muddling through your days." It's "the void between depression and flourishing." In a TED Talk, he called languishing "the dominant emotion of our time," a claim bolstered by the fact that his article went wildly viral in the weeks after it was published. The topic of "languishing" has since appeared in headlines across the Western world.[5]

As I traveled and spoke at churches and conferences, something began to happen: An audience member would approach me to ask a question or to talk after I spoke. Not long into the conversation, they would describe feeling discouraged or overwhelmed by the problems in the world and in their life. Their eyes would glint with tears, and they'd whisper, almost like a confession, "I'm just exhausted."

Burnout. Languishing. Exhaustion. These terms were helpful, and certainly part of the malaise that I and many around me were experiencing. Yet none of these terms, alone, is enough to sum up my experience. And to me, the popular solutions offered for my sense of weariness often felt shallow or futile. Experts and friends suggested increased exercise, prioritizing self-care, more vitamin B_{12} or D, mood teas, or vacations—all worthy suggestions, but none of them probed deeply enough. I felt like the Psalmist, wandering through a wasteland crying, "My soul thirsts . . . my flesh faints . . . in a dry and weary land where there is no water,"[6] and some think-piece writer would pop up from a gopher hole and yell, "But have you tried finding a better work-life balance?"

Some blamed our collective exhaustion on late capitalism or post-industrial culture—a valid point that did not actually help me. I could not suddenly retreat to a pre-industrial culture. I wasn't going to join the Amish or move off the grid (even though I sometimes fantasized about doing so). As my former realtor and current friend Shane once said between showings as I ranted about unjust markets and housing inequality, "Well, that's all true, but we can't solve capitalism today, so you still have to tell me what you want to do."

I needed something stouter and sturdier to address the aching in my soul. And I'm an Anglican priest, so I turned to the sources I knew. I slowly discovered that Christians have been writing about this twilight space between depression and flourishing for millennia. They grappled with language, reached for metaphors, and sought understanding and remedy.

My experience was echoed in the "dark night" described by the Catholic mystics John of the Cross and Teresa of Ávila.[7] The Ignatian tradition described this idea as spiritual "desolation."[8] Thinkers from the Reformed or Calvinistic traditions often named a sense of "desertion" and "drooping spirits."[9] These metaphors—desolation, dryness, drooping, darkness—point to a common human experience.

There are important nuances and differences in the way each tradition talks about these weary seasons—and academic theologians will likely wince that I'm throwing them into one big pot. But for me, discovering these ideas and these voices wasn't mainly an academic exercise—a way to better understand the finer points of historical theology. The ways Christians had discussed this very human struggle offered a kind of grammar to understand my own life. These voices helped orient me. They told me that I wasn't alone.

What I found is that the holiest people in Christianity's history, across time and cultures, have returned, again and again, to a common question: How do I keep going? Our older brothers and sisters, those who've gone before us, were not always full of ardor, and God often felt distant. In life and in faith, they were not always sure what to do or how to go on. They failed. They flailed. They doubted. They felt like giving up. Yet they found a way through to flourishing, to hope, to abundance, and they left a record for us of what they discovered.

III.

I have an acquaintance who teaches theology in a Canadian seminary. He told me recently that his goal is not so much to stir his eager young seminary students into a greater feeling of zeal, but to give them the practices and tools they need to still be following Jesus at age eighty—after suffering, doubt, ministry, and their own sins have beaten them down. But he feels that this, in a Western context, makes him a little bit of a revolutionary.

It's a revolution I think we need.

Revivalism has warped religious faith in America, perhaps especially in the peculiar and diverse movement called evangelicalism. The point of revivalism is to get people to walk the aisle, to "make a decision for Christ." It's why we love conversion stories and emotional responses to God. We are rightly moved when we hear about how people were once lost and now are found. These are great stories!

Lately, there's also an increasing popularity of deconversion stories. These are accounts of people "seeing the light" and leaving the faith in one way or another. They shed, for instance, their fundamentalist past for progressive politics, or a pastiche of spiritualities, or a contented agnosticism.

What our culture—and what the church—tends to lack are stories of a long, steady continuation in faith. We revel in newness and youthful passion. We might even occasionally laud the wisdom of years—the sages, the gurus, the living legends. But we don't have categories for the prolonged middle, for the slog, especially if this slog is accompanied by the feeling of abandonment by or distance from God. Here's the thing, though: We cannot get from newfound ardor to tried and tested wisdom without the winding middle.

This book is about the perseverance it takes not just to endure but to embrace the middle. It is about what the Christian tradition often called fortitude but we now more commonly name resilience. Perseverance and resilience are unsung virtues, not nearly as splashy as courage or justice. They can seem tired or uninteresting—the "eat your vegetables" of the spiritual life. But I have come to believe that perseverance is the most vital quality in a lifetime of discipleship, that grit is an essential ingredient of grace, and that resilience is indispensable if we are to become who we are made to be. What I need, and what I long for, are stories of *re*conversion; of coming back to Jesus, day by day, over a lifetime; of being lost and found and lost and found, again and again. I want to learn from those who have slowly discovered the long way to what lasts.

In our culture of efficiency and instant gratification, nearly everything wars against the slow, quiet virtues we need to persevere in a long apprenticeship to Jesus. We, in the contemporary Western world, are rich in comforts and graces—modern medicine, entertainment at the push of a button, relative prosperity. But we are poor in meaning, in wisdom, in relationships, in community, in a sense of purpose. I suspect this is part of why we see such widespread cultural exhaustion. We collectively lack a framework for what Thomas Aquinas called "arduous goods,"[10] those things that imbue our lives with meaning but also make them more difficult, those sturdy commitments that cost us something, that interrupt our ease and add friction to our days—the common kinds of "doing good" that make us weary.

My friend Valerie, a social worker and therapist, mentioned in passing one day that burnout fascinates her because it doesn't arise from doing the things we hate. If we hated the things that depleted us—say, how I feel about doing calculus—we'd easily leave them behind. More often, the things in life that feel most exhausting and even depleting are the things we most love, though in times of weariness, that sense of love often feels barely detectable. What is most arduous are often the deepest and most meaningful "goods" in our lives—our commitments to marriage and children or to celibacy, to our close family and friends, to service of our community and church, to creative work, and to our pursuit of God.

Perhaps as a culture we recognize, or even extol, the goodness of perseverance and resilience in theory, but we often don't understand how they are formed in us, or what that process feels like in the course of a life. This is why, I suspect, we create montages in film. Any movie where someone must grow or change likely has one (and I adore them, so it is generally my favorite part of the movie). Take, for example, perhaps the most famous one: the montage from the 1976 film *Rocky*. We know that Rocky can't simply waltz into fight after fight and easily win. We want to see him struggle and persevere. We want to watch him sacrifice time and comfort to train and develop. We want to see him, determined, weary, and covered in sweat, triumphantly running up the stairs of the Philadelphia Museum of Art. But in reality, offscreen, those long stretches of painful growth feel tedious and slow—which is why we speed them up and set them to music.

Our lives cannot be montaged. (And sadly, there is no upbeat soundtrack backing us as we try to make it through another week.) To be in the midst of the long training is to feel a bit lost, to be uncertain that anything much is happening, to be unsure of what's ahead. We feel incomplete, disoriented, or discouraged, and we aren't sure how long it will take to get to some better next scene.

Only then can we learn perseverance and resilience. But we cannot grow strong in this way—in faith, work, or love—by sheer will. We cannot simply gut out life. We need the practices, dispositions, and understanding that form us into people capable of resilience.

This book is a search for those forgotten habits and practices that deepen us in faith over time; it is a survey of historic voices who mapped the stages and stretches of the Christian life; and it is an exploration of the gifts that can only be found when we are no longer quite sure how to keep going. In these pages, I'm pulling from voices across time, cultures, and various Christian traditions—from ancient monks to Reformed preachers, from popes and poets, from saints and sinners—all who faced the void of weariness, torpor, or dullness and left behind wisdom in their wakes. I'm setting out a display table, or a kind of theological storehouse, full of resources for resilience that I discovered when I most needed them.

I return most often to a particular set of voices from around 1,700 years ago: a group of wild, surprising, and subversive men and women, ascetics and oddballs, who flourished in some of the most uninhabitable places on earth.

IV.

In the third and fourth centuries, the earliest Christian monks left the cities and towns where they lived and moved to the desolate expanses of Syria, Palestine, and especially Egypt. We now refer to these men and women as the Desert Fathers and Mothers.

By the mid-fourth century, there were thousands of them living in simplicity, usually alone or with a handful of others, in caves or small huts. We know hardly any of their names. We know relatively few details about their daily lives. They were mostly obscure and ordinary men and women. But their movement ended up changing the world.

Their lives were marked by repetitive rhythms of prayer and work—*ora et labora,* as the monastic saying goes. They prayed the Psalms, fasted often, and meditated on long passages of scripture that they'd memorized. They also wove baskets and ropes or took up other types of labor. They understood this practical work to be essential to their spiritual lives, inseparable from prayer or confession.[11] Their daily pattern of embracing both prayer and work formed their rule of life and set the cadence of their time, and they kept at that rule and cadence, year after year, decade after decade.

Most of the Desert Fathers and Mothers were former shepherds or traders who never learned to read or write. But a few, like Abba Arsenius and Evagrius of Pontus, were wealthy enough before fleeing to the desert to have been educated.[12] Those who were literate wrote down the sayings, stories, and proverbs that had been passed around this community.

Two millennia later, I live in a house where books line the walls and are stacked by the bed, discarded on the back of the toilet tank, and piled on side tables. It's Marie Kondo's house of horrors. One day, during this season of burnout, my eye fell on a paperback copy of these sayings from the Desert Fathers and Mothers. I had briefly heard about these early monks in seminary, and over the years, I had read a bit from them. I knew they were strange and mystical and interesting, so I picked up the book and started reading. This time, I couldn't stop.

Three things were clear: First, these were the weirdest people I'd ever encountered. Second, they understood what languishing, boredom, and burnout felt like, and they wrote about these experiences in ways that felt surprisingly contemporary. And finally, I sensed that they understood, in a way that I did not, what was happening inside of me and could tutor me in how to sustain a vibrant faith in the second half of my life.

These men and women were strange and wild, even in their day—and certainly in ours. They desired to give their whole lives to God, and they did so more wholeheartedly than most of us ever will. Some fought with demons (they meant this literally) or occasionally had visions. Most of them fasted for days and often spoke in symbols, metaphors, and parables. They were radicals and nonconformists, just a touch punk rock.

And they were revered by early Christians. Without wanting to be, some became spiritual celebrities. Men and women would flock to them, some traveling for days into the desert, wanting advice and wisdom. At times, even emperors would seek them out.[13] They responded graciously to guests but were also sometimes a little annoyed. (If in an introverted moment you have pretended not to notice an acquaintance in a crowded coffee shop, imagine if you moved to a cave in the desert to be alone and people still didn't take the hint.) Some went to extremes to seek solitude and silence. Simeon the Stylite, who became something of a legend in the fifth century, took up residence on a pillar sixty or seventy feet above ground to escape the crowds of pilgrims seeking his advice.[14] (Talk about going off-grid!)

Part of what made me so hungry to learn from these early monks is that they are so radically outside my moment and culture. At a time when the Western world, and even the church, is polarizing, these voices are completely different from both modern religious conservatism and progressivism, free of much of the baggage of our contemporary culture wars. They were profoundly human, with profoundly relatable struggles. Yet they offered me a fresh, countercultural perspective that sounded nothing like what I could find on social media, in the "Christian Living" section of my local bookstore, or in the latest self-help trend.

Their sayings are immensely practical. Though they cared about doctrine and scripture, their sayings focus not so much on teasing out finer points of theology, but instead on what discipleship looks and feels like in real time. They examined the temptations we encounter and how best to battle them. When Christians refer to the early church fathers, we usually mean those who helped form the core doctrines of the faith—who shaped our understanding of the Trinity, who hammered out the great creeds. But the Desert Fathers and Mothers are, in some sense, not so much the midwives of Christian doctrine but of Christian practice. Their movement birthed global monasticism and has profoundly influenced Christian spirituality, even for those of us who live in suburbs and cities, work jobs, and seek to live faithfully in the twenty-first century.

To be sure, these men and women were not infallible. I find some of their sayings and advice baffling, or simply wrong. And I'm not about to go live atop a sixty-foot pillar. But there are moments when I catch myself grinning at how connected I feel to the Desert Fathers and Mothers across seventeen centuries. They fled city life to get away from temptations and spiritual desolation, only to discover that all their temptations, neuroses, compulsions, insecurities, and woundedness remained present inside of them. They escaped society, but they soon realized they could not escape themselves. Their problems followed them wherever they went. This realization transformed them.

Removed from the workaday world, they became something akin to advanced research scientists delving into the human condition, with their own interior lives as their chief subject. They spent their days noticing the subtleties and progression of the Christian life. Like spiritual physicians, they worked diagnostically, studying what was disordered within themselves and seeking out ways of remedy and redemption. Out of that study and experience came a profound self-awareness and understanding of humanity.

In the time and culture of these early monks, the desert was not just a physical place but a psychological reality, an *internal* landscape.[15] In the scriptures, the desert (sometimes translated as "the wilderness") is where people contend with God and with evil. It's where Jacob wrestled with the angel of the Lord. It's where the Israelites wandered for decades. It's where Jesus was tempted by the devil.

In spite of—or, more likely, *because* of—their spiritually difficult and ascetic lives, these early monks and mystics had intense seasons of languishing, weariness, and a sense of God's distance. They began to name this experience after the arid landscape in which they had chosen to live. They called it "aridity."[16]

Discovering this term gave shape to these times when prayer feels unsatisfying and life, in general, feels hard. Aridity named a deeper spiritual reality beneath my vague sense of malaise and weariness. It helped describe the landscape of my soul.

For an experience so commonly discussed since the earliest days of the church, this concept was strangely absent from my own understanding of the Christian life. I had not been warned about long seasons of spiritual drought and disorientation. I had not been told that this was an inevitable—even necessary—part of the Christian life, so when I encountered it, I felt afraid and uncertain. I wondered if this was evidence I had done something wrong or evidence that faith may not be worth keeping.

The Desert Fathers and Mothers, however, show us in their words and in their lives that the desert is not something to be feared. "The desert is a necessary stage on the spiritual journey," writes the Orthodox theologian John Chryssavgis. "To avoid it would be harmful. To dress it up or conceal it may be tempting; but it also proves destructive in the spiritual path."[17]

Our consumer culture demands convenience, efficiency, and ease. When God seems distant, we want him to show off for us and make himself known.* We want the secret knowledge or program that will unlock all our potential and free us from difficulties, desolation, and death. We want a strategy and plan that will make the good in our life not so arduous. Offering the promise of this, even in the spiritual life, is the way to make faith marketable. It is not, however, the way to make disciples.

To everyone's disappointment, there is no secret knowledge. There is no spiritual or emotional shortcut where we skip over the long way of practice into perpetual contentment, joy, and awe. There are no cheat codes in the Christian life. And there's no shortcut in the desert. We must go through it, not around it.

* I will follow scripture and the majority of the Christian tradition in using male pronouns when referring to God. I understand that God is not a biological male, and that both men and women are equally made in the image of God. However, avoiding pronouns altogether leads to clunky phrasing and impersonal language about God. (In this sentence, for example, I would have had to use the neologism "Godself.") I acknowledge the limitations that the English language imposes and ask for grace from readers who find the use of male pronouns difficult.

V.

On a cold afternoon at the tail end of the year, I went on a long walk with my close friend Hannah, who is also a trained spiritual director. I told her about the Desert Fathers and Mothers. I talked to her about the past few years of weariness and aridity. She said something like, "Oh, honey, this is an important season, but you can't simply white-knuckle your way through it, keeping at your duty. You have to find the invitation for you in this time. What is God inviting you into?"

The desert, to steal a phrase from theologian Stanley Hauerwas, is for learning "how to go on when you don't know where you are."[18] In order to learn this, we must find the invitation for us in these seasons when prayer, work, and relationships feel harder than we think they should.

Jonathan and I have a phrase that we say in moments of difficulty or struggle: "Numb out, flame out, or go deep." As life stretches on and we begin, more and more, to meet with suffering, sadness, or simply the cussedness of daily living, I've come to think that people can respond in these three ways.

To flame out is the most dramatic option. This is when people, feeling trapped, try to escape by exploding their own lives without much thought of the collateral damage. This is the stuff that people gossip about: the affairs, the arrests, the public meltdowns, the scandals. I have a friend, a once-married pastor, who went to a conference, met a woman, slept with her, and eventually left his wife, their baby and toddler, and an entire community in tatters. He was in real pain and wanted out, so he blew up his life and the lives of those around him. He flamed out.

To numb out, the most common response, is when we simply anesthetize ourselves through food, drink, work, shopping, screens, or other easy comforts. It's the little avoidances, the little addictions, the little denials that build a pattern. It's the couple that dutifully sticks out their marriage but settles for years of silent, embittered apathy. It's when you stop really living, stop really feeling, stop really hoping or dreaming or grieving, and instead settle for a long slide into oblivion. It's when you grow cold or bitter and withdraw into yourself. I have a friend who cannot be alone with her thoughts. She falls asleep to television. She fills the air with background noise, podcasts that she doesn't actually hear. One way or another, she makes sure that she never has to be alone in a quiet room, never has to feel the losses and anxieties in her life, never has to face her sorrows or regrets. She numbs out.

And then, by God's grace, there's the third option: Go deep. To go deep into God, into mystery, into self-understanding, into repentance, into relationships with others, into the practice of faith. Deep into grace.

To go deep means looking with unflinching honesty at the truth of things—the pain in our lives, the sins and weaknesses in ourselves and those around us. It means learning to receive anew the love of God and the rich goodness of life. To go deep requires us to remain with difficult questions, relationships, practices, and commitments, while also remaining alive to God and to ourselves. It requires us to learn to exist, and to thrive, in places of incompleteness, unfulfillment, liminality, and uncertainty.

The invitation that comes in the deserts of our lives is to go deep. It's the only way to survive them intact.

We don't have to seek out the literal desert like the Desert Fathers and Mothers did. The desert comes for us all. Maybe it looks like disappointment, suffering, or burnout. Or like a profound sense of disorientation, doubt, or God's distance. Maybe it looks like church hurt, marital difficulties, or frustration in our work.[19]

When we meet the desert, we can try to avoid it through numbing, chasing little and big pleasures that hollow us out over time. Or we can throw off our beliefs, obligations, and responsibilities, becoming agents of chaos to those around us. Or we can learn to keep going when we don't know where we are; we can submit to the discipline of the desert, accepting its trials as the strange way that the weary find rest, embracing its desolation as the very place that we learn to grow.

This is the invitation I found in the desert. This is the path I'm seeking to discover. And this book is the field notes on what I've found.

2

Stay in Your Cell

stability in practice

I.

I grow achingly sad at times that the good things in my life are arduous. I procrastinate and grumble about my work. I get bored of and cynical about spiritual things. I resent that I have to call my mom back or listen to my kid tell an interminable story or sit through a sermon or pray for my enemies or say hello to my neighbors. I get overwhelmed by the number of texts or emails I receive in a day, and the number of needs in the world—and even in just my own home. I do not want to try. I do not want to love or care. I protest. I form a picket line in my front yard—me, alone, marching in a circle, with a sandwich board: "What do I want? Ease! When do I want it? Now and forever!"

In these moments, I am facing an ancient temptation that the Desert Fathers and Mothers named as the meanest and most difficult to resist: *acedia*. This word, acedia, is listed by early Christians as one of the "eight bad thoughts," or eight "pressures on the soul," which later evolved into the more familiar seven deadly sins.[1] It lacks a dynamically equivalent translation in English. It is often translated (inadequately) as "sloth." But it does not always look like ignoring the dishes to cuddle up with a family-size bag of Doritos and binge-watch for hours.

Instead, it has to do with an internal state of restlessness, boredom, cynicism, and futility. It is a lack of motivation. Translated literally, it means "lack of care."[2] My favorite definition, however, comes from John Paul II: "a sadness arising from the fact that the good is difficult."[3]

Aridity and acedia are not the same thing. Aridity is more like a spiritual environment—a season of disorientation when we sense God's absence, even if we still feel desire for God. But in that spiritual biome, certain temptations tend to shoot up like weeds. In these seasons of languishing, when prayer and work feel difficult, the temptation to acedia is most fierce and nearly always at hand. When I am in the throes of acedia, I catch myself believing that the only way I can be free from my sense of weariness and dullness is to have no demands on me, at all.

Acedia is constantly discussed in the monastic tradition. It is "the monk's temptation," writes Kathleen Norris in her classic book *Acedia & Me,* "because, in a demanding life of prayer, it offers the ease of indifference. Yet I have come to believe that acedia can strike anyone whose work requires self-motivation and solitude, anyone who remains married 'for better or for worse,' anyone who is determined to stay true to a commitment that is sorely tested in everyday life."[4]

Both aridity and acedia make life—particularly the life of faith—feel impossible and unfulfilling. Both are impediments to prayer. And in the monastic tradition, they both have the same treatment: When desert monks wanted to abandon their times of regular prayer, silence, and solitude, when they were tempted to "flee from the arena" and give up their spiritual battle, the advice given over and over was: *Stay in your cell.*[5]

Abba Arsenius advised a struggling monk: "Go, eat, drink and sleep, only do not leave your cell."[6] The word *cell* comes from the Latin word simply meaning "a small room." For the Desert Fathers and Mothers, it was the cave or hut, in which one prays and works.

For these desert monks, "stay in your cell" literally meant stay in your room and persist in your daily habits of prayer and work. It was a call to be steadfast regardless of how you feel.[7]

In his rule, Saint Benedict expanded "staying in the cell" into the idea of *stabilitas,* or stability—one of three vows that Benedictine monks take even today.[8] Drawing from the Desert Fathers and Mothers, it is a vow to stay in place, to stay with a particular monastic community, to stay true to one's commitments, and to keep at the monk's practices of prayer, work, and worship.

Benedict instructed monks in training to count the cost—to consider "all the hard and the rough things through which lies the way to God"—and only then to respond by taking up stability, which is the way of perseverance.[9] Monks in this tradition later developed the idea of *stabilitas cordis*—stability of the heart—to highlight how stability is not just remaining in a particular location but is, more profoundly, the cultivation of deep spiritual rootedness and resilience.[10]

The way to walk in faith today is the way Christians have, more or less, sustained the faith for two thousand years: practices like prayer and fasting, silence and solitude, study of and meditation on the scriptures, gathered worship, the sacraments, repentance, obedience, generosity, and love of neighbor. These all involve repetition, failure, renewal, perseverance, and hard-won wisdom. They will all feel slow and take time, which is why, more than any new strategy, plan, app, or insight, what we most need to sustain a life of faithfulness is to learn the practices of stability.

The desert call to stay in one's cell is an invitation to the deep internal work that only happens in us with patience, struggle, and perseverance. "Away, enter your cell and sit down," said Abba Moses, "and your cell will teach you everything."[11] Whether or not we have a literal monastic cell, this is an invitation to all of us.

II.

When things seemed most unfulfilling amid my desert season, I flew to Wichita to speak at a conference and heard a lecture by the writer Jen Pollock Michel on keeping at faith when our lives feel difficult and spiritual things feel empty. It was one of those talks that seem to speak directly to you, even though you're sitting in a crowd of hundreds.

Michel said that we resist thinking of faith in terms of habits and practices because as a culture we are "afraid of performativity." We don't like going through the motions. We want life and faith to feel vibrant and passionate. We want to feel on fire. This leads us to "favor feelings of faith over and against its ordinary, everyday practices." But what do we do, she asked, in those times when a gap grows between "the moods of faith and the motions—the habits—of faith?"[12]

We often assume that we must first experience affection, wonder, or zeal toward God; then, out of those feelings, we will respond authentically in worship, prayer, or obedience. Certain kinds of churches even bake these assumptions into their worship services, adding the kick drum to a swelling crescendo during the altar call to trigger a particular emotional response. But it is usually our quiet, week in and week out practices that drive our feelings and thoughts about God, not the other way around. "When you or I are not in the mood for faith," Michel said, "we can and we must keep at its habits."[13]

This is one way that we stay in the cell.

As I was writing my last book, I wrote a sentence that I did not know I believed until I read it on the page: "Faith," I wrote, "is more craft than feeling."[14] I remember stopping to read it aloud, trying to decide if it was true. It was a small sentence in a long book, but this analogy would soon slowly make its way through each room in my house, each relationship I had, each prayer I prayed, each hour of my day.

The analogy of craft helped me because I understood, not so much as a Christian but as a writer, that creative inspiration—the elusive, yet much discussed, state of "flow"—is painfully rare.[15] One learns pretty quickly that the craft cannot be sustained by peak moments of inspiration and brilliance. Those moments, as profound and powerful as they are, do not a writer make. Most artists I know have long swaths of time—years, even—when they feel about as enthusiastic about their work as they do about stubbing their toe. But a writer *writes.* A painter paints. A musician makes music.

Anne Lamott's well-known advice to writers has nothing to do with internal feelings or enthusiasm: "How to write: Butt in chair. Start each day anywhere. Let yourself do it badly. Just take one passage at a time. Get butt back in chair."[16] It's habits. It's practices. It's repetition. If one ever arrives at anything like flow, it is because of countless days, weeks, and years of ordinary disciplines that, in the moment anyway, seem frustrating, faltering, and like nothing significant is happening.

The writers of scripture often speak about faith as a kind of exercise or craft. The apostle Paul talks about training in godliness the same way athletes train in a sport. He reminds the church in Philippi that everything they have heard from him they must "put . . . into practice."[17] He tells Timothy to "practice" the faith he's been given, so that others can "see your progress" in it. He tells him this will require repetition and persistence.[18]

We tend to use the word *faith* to mean cognitive assent to a set of propositional truths or having certain spiritual experiences. But the idea of faith as a craft reminds us that faith involves the reorientation and transformation of how we use our days, our time, our attention, and our bodies; it asks us not just to examine our thinking but our habits as well.

Church, then, is not simply a place to receive information. It is a place of formation. In church, we learn the habits that are meant to mark our daily lives. We learn to apologize to our kids on Wednesday by practicing communal confession on our knees each Sunday. We learn to practice silent prayer through moments of silence together each week. We learn to pray by reciting the Psalms together. We learn the practices of faith as a community gathered, and we continue them in our own ways in our work, homes, families, and neighborhoods.[19]

This does not mean that our thinking or doctrine or emotions do not matter—these all matter. But the (albeit imperfect) analogy of faith as a craft has allowed me to embrace small, daily work—even times of drudgery—without losing the vision of something greater. After all, a writer does not take up her pen *because* writing is arduous. She is after something more: truth, beauty, illumination, transcendence. But the way that looks each day is simply: butt in chair.

Understanding faith as a craft does not mean that our life in Christ is not completely led, from beginning to end, by grace. We do not stay at the practices of faith because we hope to eke out approval from a disappointed God or because we are trying to catch the attention of a withholding taskmaster. The capacity to persist in practices of faith is a gift freely given.

At the same time, grace is not a magic trick. It does not zap us into a new way of being but instead invites our participation. As we cooperate with God's work in us and in the world, grace transforms us, grabbing hold of us from within and reorienting our whole selves.

Growing in a craft, of any kind, involves struggle and change. And if life itself—including work, marriage, parenting, friendship, love, and Christian discipleship—is a kind of craft, we can have hope that if something feels difficult, even profoundly so, it is not necessarily because we are doing it wrong or because the thing we are attempting isn't worthy.

When Abba Arsenius instructed a younger monk to stay in his cell, he was not asking him to gin up more emotion or spiritual ardor. He was not telling him to feel anything at all. Nor was he shaming him for his struggles, blaming him for a lack of faith. But neither did he instruct him to knock off prayer and work, indulge his distractions and fantasies, and find his own way. He instead told the struggling monk to feel boredom, to take care of his daily needs—"eat, drink and sleep"—and, above all, to keep at his rhythms of prayer and work, to continue in the long craft of faith.

III.

"In working-class France, when an apprentice got hurt, or when he got tired," writes Annie Dillard, "the experienced workers said, 'It is the trade entering his body.'" She continues, "Cell by cell, molecule by molecule, atom by atom, part of the brain changes physical shape to accommodate" a craft.[20]

Craft shapes our bodies, how we use our very skin and bones. "Butt in chair" is a thoroughly embodied idea.

And when it comes to the craft of faith, the same is true. When we feel we cannot pray, our bodies often lead the way. "You can lift up your hands regardless of how you feel," writes Eugene Peterson, reflecting on Psalm 134's call to lift up our hands in worship. "It is a simple motor movement. You may not be able to command your heart, but you can command your arms."[21]

People often end up at my Anglican church when they are no longer sure how to pray. Suffering, aridity, or simply the slog of normal life has brought them to the place where emotional or intellectual ardor alone is not enough to sustain them. They don't have the energy to conjure up a particular internal experience in their Sunday worship service. But they want to continue to follow Jesus. They know they cannot command their hearts, but they can command their arms, and they would like to be told what to do with them. They would like to be taught how to worship with their bodies.

In the liturgy, we make the sign of the cross, we lift up our hands to receive a blessing, we pass the peace, we receive Communion, we pray prayers that we've been given. However I may feel about prayer on any given Sunday, I kneel. I bend my knees. And if my heart will not submit to God, my body leads the way. I take the Eucharist, and even if I cannot feel the presence of Christ, I receive him in my hands, on my tongue.

Prayer, for the Desert Fathers and Mothers, was an embodied exercise. To stay in the cell meant not just to embrace a certain frame of mind but, very concretely, to kneel or stand for regular times of prayer in a particular place, to pray or sing the Psalms (usually aloud), to lift one's hands. When someone asked Abba Macarius how to pray, he replied, "There is no need at all to make long discourses. It is enough to stretch out one's hands and to say: 'Lord, as you will, and as you know, have mercy.' "[22]

Pray with your body at certain times each day, and your soul eventually catches up. Peterson concludes, "Act your gratitude; pantomime your thanks; you will become that which you do."[23]

This is one of the gifts that perseverance gives us. When we, apprentices of Jesus, grow tired or hurt yet continue in these practices of faith, I like to think that the pain we experience is the feeling of the craft of faith no longer hovering on the surface of our hearts and emotional lives, but slowly entering into our very bodies.

IV.

The Life of Antony, a fourth-century book about perhaps the most famous Desert Father, contains a strange and disturbing story. Antony was one of the first monks to move into the Egyptian desert to devote his life to prayer. When he was thirty-five years old, living among the tombs outside of his village on the Nile, he encountered demons who beat him brutally. He was broken and in pain, nearly to the point of death. Yet he fought on. Eventually, as Antony fought back, the Lord came to his aid—in the story, Antony sees a beam of light and the demons flee. Panting and out of breath, Antony asks God, quite understandably, "Where were you? Why didn't you appear in the beginning, so that you could stop my distresses?"

A voice comes to him: "I was here, Antony, but I waited to watch your struggle."[24]

Suffice it to say, I have never been in a fistfight with demons, nor has anyone I've ever met. (There's a lot of incredibly strange stuff in *The Life of Antony*.) But all of us can likely relate to feeling beaten down by the darkness and evil in the world, the anxieties and compulsions within us, the complexities and difficulties around us. All of us have had times when we long for God to show up, to show himself, to make things easier, but feel that God hangs back, silent and distant. All of us have had times when we feel bruised and bloodied by life and we ask God, "Where are you? Why are you nowhere to be found?"

God's answer to Antony in this story is hard for me to take. "I waited to watch your struggle." *What kind of answer is that?!* It makes

God seem like an aloof jerk, or a middle school bully, sitting idly by while a kid gets pounded.

Yet plainly, if we look at our lives, there are times that feel burdensome, brutal, or wearying, and relief does not come quickly. When God seems to disappear or hang back, is it negligence? Is it cruelty? And if not, then what's the purpose? Why would anyone who loves us watch us struggle?

One answer comes from John of the Cross, a monk from sixteenth-century Spain, in his famous "dark night of the soul," an idea I misunderstood until recently. I thought of "the dark night" as an acute season of suffering—those times when we face life's deepest tragedies. But that's not primarily how John describes it.

As a monk, John of the Cross became known for his mystical encounters with Jesus and his spiritual insight. He and his friend Teresa of Ávila together sought to reform monastic life in Spain, but (perhaps unsurprisingly) some powerful people didn't like his agitation, and his efforts eventually landed him in prison.[25] From that quite literally dark place of isolation and suffering, he set out to write a guide to how we progress in the spiritual life. He wanted to map out the terrain of spiritual growth, both for beginners and for what he called "proficients." He wanted to warn of its pitfalls and guide others on the way.

When we first come to faith, John explains, God often gets us going through a sense of sweetness and exhilaration—what John calls "illumination." It's the same energy we associate with so many beginnings—young love, a new adventure, the start of an exciting creative project. When a soul is first "converted to the service of God," he writes, it is "as a rule, spiritually nurtured and caressed by God, even as is the tender child by its loving mother."[26] Prayer and worship feel ardent. The spiritual life is abundant and intriguing. God seems plain to see. We feel passionate and alive. Work, relationships, and faith feel exciting.

Christians throughout church history, particularly mystics, tell this story often: God gives consolation after consolation—visions, miracles, certainty, a palpable sense of his closeness—to get people going in their life of faith. And then, the resistance increases. The training wheels come off. Things suddenly feel arduous and disorienting. This is the dark night. John of the Cross describes it as a time when we sense spiritual abandonment and a loss of meaning. He specifically calls this a time of aridity.[27]

Just as seeking "flow" does not sustain a craft, John says that seeking "consolation" in the spiritual life is not what forms disciples. As great as times of "sweetness" may be, they carry a temptation: to seek God merely for "spiritual pleasures," which John says can morph into "spiritual avarice."[28] We want a relationship with God to feel easy and fulfilling and to meet our felt needs. We want God to come like a hero in a cape to rescue us from difficulties, from a life that feels arduous, disappointing, or monotonous. We subtly begin to treat faith as a hit or a high, and ultimately, a consumer product. We lurch from spiritual fad to spiritual fad, looking for something that works for us and that makes our life work.

John understood that devotion itself could be co-opted into consumerism long before Instagram influencers, conference headliners, and faith-based "content creators" promised to revolutionize our spiritual lives with devotional apps, podcasts, and self-help books. He describes people who "expend all their effort in seeking spiritual pleasure and consolation." They never tire "of reading books and they begin, now one meditation, now another, in their pursuit of this pleasure which they desire to experience in the things of God."[29]

Certainly, in our culture, there are still many—both in the church and outside it—who chase the next spiritual trend. People have built whole careers by offering half-baked spiritual novelties, self-empowerment, and self-transformation. But John is skeptical of this. It's not that books (ahem . . . like this one) or devotionals or conferences are bad, but that, as my friend's mentor once pointed out to him, we have cultivated "an insatiable appetite for the interesting."

To continue being formed in apprenticeship to Christ, we must learn to set aside what John of the Cross calls our "swaddling clothes" and come to God, not for certain spiritual feelings, highs, or insight, but merely for God himself.[30] In order for us to grow in this way, God allows the sense of his presence to lessen. From our vantage point, it seems as if he withdraws. It seems he's sitting back and watching us struggle.

For those, like me, who were subtly (or not so subtly) taught that our subjective experience of God determines the sincerity of our faith, this resistance and difficulty in the spiritual life is disorienting. It's difficult to believe that this isn't a punishment of some sort, a divine response to our sin. And indeed, John warned us that there will be Christians who insist that it is. When God leads us down a "path of dark contemplation and aridity," he writes, we will inevitably meet others who blame the problem on temperament.[31] They will tell us to cheer up, to look on the bright side, to stay positive. Some will assume that spiritual emptiness can only arise from personal failure or hidden sin.

Yet John sees the dark night as an *essential* stage of growth that brings new progress in knowing God. It is not a failure of apprenticeship. It is the apprenticeship.

The shadow side of zeal and enthusiasm is that they can teach us to approach life valuing only those things that make us feel good, those things that excite us and reaffirm our strengths. We value our children to the extent that they make us smile and make us proud, to the extent that they prove we are good parents who've done a good job forming such lovely people. But when they seem to hold up a mirror to our worst qualities, when they need a love from us that we find ourselves incapable of giving, we start to resent them. We come to our spouse and our marriage to make us happy, to make us feel okay and fulfilled, and when they fail us, we withdraw into bitterness or question whether there's any value in continuing in our commitment. We approach friends looking for them to cure our loneliness, to make us laugh or make us feel special, or give us the thrill of knowing someone interesting or fun, and when they frustrate us or bore us or want more from us than we can give, we ghost them. And we come to God asking him to prove his worth to us by making faith feel fruitful, moving, or passionate and by rescuing us from struggle and pain. That's his job, right?

In this way of living, things and people—even God—don't hold value in and of themselves. They hold value to the extent that they are useful to us. And whether we approach a mountain range, a friend, or the divine this way, it is inherently exploitative. It is inherently an assault on stability of the heart.

This is how, very often, I have lived. I come looking for a spirituality that works for me. I expect God to be an ally in my quest for an ever-fulfilling life.

V.

When my daughter was just over two, I decided it was time to wean her—a decision that every woman on the planet seemed to have intense opinions about in the raging age of "mommy blogs." My daughter had developed a habit of waking around three A.M. every night for her version of a DoorDash nightcap, delivered by me, her walking juice box. But with a new baby on the way, it was time for a change.

That first night of weaning, I went to sleep afraid. I worried my daughter would cry inconsolably—which would make me cry too. Sure enough, around three A.M., she began crying for me to come, and her cries grew louder and more insistent. Jonathan tried to comfort her but to no avail. He returned to our room for us to lie in the dark and fret together.

Finally he watched as I, pushover that I am, got up, slipped my most impenetrable turtleneck over my pajamas, and disappeared into our daughter's room. After another minute or so, she fell silent.

When I came back to bed a while later, Jonathan, still awake, whispered, "Did you cave?" He assumed her silence meant I'd nursed her. But no, I told him. I'd sat with her, gently stroking her wispy baby hair. She curled up close against my warm body and relaxed. She didn't need the milk. She just needed me. "That's beautiful," he said.

Something changed in my relationship with my daughter that night. She was still utterly dependent on me. But something new emerged.

In Psalm 131, the Psalmist writes, "I have stilled and quieted my soul; like a weaned child with his mother, like a weaned child is my soul within me."[32] For years, I resisted the metaphor. I'd ask people: Why a *weaned* child? Isn't an unweaned child closer, more dependent, more connected, more enamored with their mother? I asked scholars this. I asked bishops. They all said something profound like, "Huh, I've never thought about it." (Maybe normal people don't dwell on the intricacies of breastfeeding metaphors as much as I do.)[33]

But those wee hours with my daughter showed me something. A weaned child relaxes in the presence of her mother because she is not after anything the mother can give her, but has instead learned to enjoy her mother for the mother's own sake.

And this is the shift John of the Cross says that the dark night brings in our souls. It teaches us, in John's words, to practice the love of God, since it is "not now moved by the pleasure of attraction and sweetness which it finds . . . but only by God."[34]

In those dark hours, we feel—maybe like my daughter did—abandoned. We feel God does not hear us or does not know what we need. We may grow angry that he is withholding good things from us, that he is watching us struggle. But he's listening to every cry and every call. He's responding to us in a way we do not recognize and have not known before.

What made John of the Cross a saint? Was it his early ecstasies? Or was it that, by God's persistent but painful grace, he kept going through the dark night?

The point of the dark night, like the experience of aridity, is not to simply get through it as soon as possible. The point is not to find the right formula to escape it or skip over it. The point is to surrender to God's work in the midst of it. John says it is meant to teach us "fortitude" and steadfastness.[35] It is meant to teach us to persevere in practices and habits of faith. It is meant to teach us stability of the heart.

God gets us going with fireworks, but we grow deep when the craft of faith becomes dull or difficult. This is when we learn to love God, not because we have to, not because he makes things work for us, not because he gives us pleasure, but for God's own sake. Our soul grows quiet like the Psalmist's. The cacophony within us settles, and we slowly, painfully, release the imagined good life that we once demanded and learn to cling to God himself.

VI.

God, in his kindness, is not committed to my ease or to my desires. But God is committed to me—to my salvation, my healing, my wholeness, my joy, my strengthening, my deepening. Resilience is not just a means to an end—the way of getting through a difficult experience. It is a necessary part of becoming who we must become. But it can only be learned in the struggle.

This is why we stay in our cell.

It's become the mantra of my life, the words Jonathan and I remind each other of constantly. In a week where doubt roars loud, faith feels weak, and prayer feels pointless: Just stay in the cell, we'll say. Keep praying, keep lifting your hands and bending your knees, keep meditating on the Psalms, keep practicing silence, leaning in with expectation and longing. A horrible argument with our teenage daughter? Just stay in the cell. Keep trying. Keep loving, caring, praying, forgiving, learning, repenting, and believing the best of her. A hard conversation with a church member? Just stay in your cell. Stay in the friendship, keep showing up to church, to others, to awkward conversations. A miserable few days of writing or marriage or work or grief? Stay in the cell. Don't flame out. Don't numb out and drift away. Stay in the place you are in. Feel all the feelings you are feeling. And be willing to remain in the incompleteness, the disorientation, the disappointment, and the disciplines of your life.

The struggling monk whom Abba Arsenius encouraged to "eat, drink and sleep, only do not leave your cell" listened. He remained in his community and gave himself to quotidian practices of faith and work—trimming palm leaves, reading, singing Psalms, praying. There were no fireworks, no visions, no flow. He simply did what was at hand to do. He stayed in his cell.

We don't know much about his life. We don't even know his name. But in the sayings of the Desert Fathers and Mothers, his story ends with these hopeful and humble words, which have become a kind of prayer for me, a handhold on a hard climb: "And so by God's help he went on little by little until he had indeed become what he was meant to become."[36]

His cell taught him everything.

3

Pledge Your Body to the Walls

stability in commitments and community

I.

For decades, my husband and I moved too much, pinballing between five U.S. states in our first fifteen years of marriage.

We relocated to go to seminary. We relocated so Jonathan could get a PhD. We relocated for new jobs. We relocated to be closer to family. But we never stayed anywhere for long. Looking back, much of the motivation for our migratory and mobile life was a quest for the next opportunity—a new career, a new place, a new church, a new community. This isn't all bad, and it certainly is the norm in our rootless culture. Yet living this way subtly trained us to look to external changes to bring resolution to the problems of our life. Maybe the next church would bring a more committed and loving community. Maybe the next job would make life more exciting. Maybe the next place could somehow make us kinder, more patient, more organized, more joyful people. There was always the possibility of some quick resolution just over the horizon.

Around the time I turned forty, having longed for an elusive stability for many years, I presented Jonathan with a list of six cities, all places near where we had friends or family. I am willing to live in any of these places, I said, but wherever you pick, we are staying for decades, and unless an angel of the Lord shows up in my bedroom or a disembodied hand scrawls writing on the wall, if you leave before then, you will be going alone. I'll visit you often, but I'm not moving again. I wasn't totally serious, but he knew I wasn't totally kidding either.

He didn't need much convincing, though. He had learned by then that we needed to seek stability.

So he chose a city from the list, and we moved back to my hometown.

When we finally stopped moving, something interesting happened. All the problems, flaws, sorrows, and limitations in our marriage, our family, our community, and ourselves became simply what they were. Our life was no longer out there somewhere, waiting to be found. It was right here, all around us.

Over the next few years, issues I thought I had left behind began bubbling up in my thoughts and emotions: a deep wound from a pastoral colleague, unforgiveness I harbored from a relationship long past, grief over losses from years before, patterns of ingratitude, anger, and impatience in my life. My newfound stability surfaced what I'd buried through distraction and mobility. And there was no longer an eject button. If I was going to see change, healing, improvement, these had to be wrought from the inside out. They had to begin here, with me, in this very place with these very people.

"We are easily persuaded that the problem of growing up in the life of the spirit can be localized—outside ourselves," writes former Archbishop of Canterbury Rowan Williams in his meditations on the Desert Fathers and Mothers. "Somewhere else I could be nicer, holier, more balanced, more detached about criticism, more disciplined, able to sing in tune and probably thinner as well."[1] The practice of stability asks us to stop looking to change our circumstances to find the good life, and to instead look to God to change and transform us.

To "stay in the cell" is not only a call to continue in prayer and other practices of faith. It is also a call to stay put. It is a call to stay in a place, in a particular community. It is a call to remain committed to the people right around us. In asking younger monks and nuns to stay in their cells, these desert elders were telling them to embrace the constraints of time, people, place, and particularity.

In the sayings of the Desert Fathers and Mothers, this insistence on staying put is pervasive and nearly constantly repeated, perhaps indicating that instability and mobility were common problems in the desert. Amma Syncletica, a Desert Mother, gives us this image: "Just as the bird who abandons the eggs she was sitting on prevents them from hatching, so the monk or nun grows cold and their faith dies, when they go around from one place to another."[2]

She suggests that something vital is gestating, being born in us, but it can only come into being if we stick with it, if we remain committed to what is growing right where we are. An anonymous monk similarly remarks, "If a trial comes upon you in the place where you live, do not leave that place. Wherever you go, you find that what you are running from is ahead of you."[3]

In composing his rule, Benedict reserved harsh criticism for *gyrovagues*, monks who drifted from region to region and monastery to monastery.[4] These wandering monks never gave themselves to any place or any community for long. Instead, they were on an endless search, looking for the perfect monastery, the perfect relationships, the perfect worship, somewhere they felt they could be most valued, most holy, most alive.

Today, consumerism has formed us all to be gyrovagues in a million large and small ways. It isn't just that people (like me) tend to move a lot. We see this impulse in the constant chase of online dating, in the easy way we switch church communities, in the preference for distant, online interactions over meeting our neighbors, in the weak family and friendship ties that have made loneliness an epidemic. To stay on the hunt, always seeking the better deal, the better community or church or job or spouse or friends, to attempt to be everywhere and nowhere at once, to keep our options ever open, is to, in the end, live a half life.

I know of a tiny church in a trendy city in the Pacific Northwest. They noticed that their town had a lot of turnover—people approached their city as consumers, enjoying its coveted job market, hip coffee shops, and cool vibe, then moving on to other places whenever they felt like it. So this congregation took a radical step. They decided to take up something like a monk's vow of stability. Their adult members voluntarily committed not to move to another place unless the congregation affirmed together that God had called someone elsewhere.

I know that this practice is shocking, maybe even alarming, in our day when individual freedom is valued above all. In a controlling or unhealthy church, it could be a practice rife with abuse, and I doubt it will ever be adopted widely (my own church has no such practice). But the impulse to seek stability as a community is a needed and faithful one, and it is worth considering what this may look like now, in practical ways, even for us non-monastics.

As disciples of Jesus, we must not live as if we are autonomous individuals with infinite options. We must allow others to lay claims on us, to limit us even. To go deep with God always involves going deep with others, being rooted in a place, a community, a tradition, a church.

Of course, terms and conditions apply. No one should feel they must stay in a marriage with an adulterous or abusive spouse, in a job with a bullying or exploitative boss, or in a church with an unethical or heretical pastor. These are tragic situations, and heartbreakingly common.

And there are certainly less dire times in which a change may be necessary. I am not saying we ought never change jobs, cities, churches, or circumstances. Clearly, even in the pages of scripture, God tells people to up and go to another place at times. There are gradients in our level of commitment—and not all things in our lives rise to the level of a vow, an obligation, or certainly a monk's rule of life. What saints of old, including the Desert Fathers and Mothers, offer us is wisdom, not law.

Still, the witness of Christians throughout history is that we ought to be skeptical of the impulse to bolt when things become arduous and difficult. Particularly in times of aridity, we need to fight the urge to flee. To follow only our bliss is to, in the end, miss everything the cell has to teach us.

I cannot tell you precisely what the cell of your life, your community, and your commitments will teach you. I do know, however, that the practice of staying forces us to look at ourselves and see ourselves clearly without giving in to the fantasy that elsewhere, we would be different. Stability teaches us that growth can only come if we remain still long enough to let our roots sink deeply into our Source, into God himself.

II.

When I was a young adult, my biggest fear was feeling stuck. I was worried that in the course of my life—which seemed all ahead of me at the time—I would come to feel regret or boredom, that I would be limited by the choices I made. In the last decade, though, I have come to believe that feeling stuck at times is not just inevitable, it is important.

The advice that a desert elder gives to a fellow monk struggling with an unnamed temptation is "Hurry! Go! Sit in your cell! Give your body as a pledge to the walls . . ."[5]

We come to a point, often but not always around midlife, when the decisions we have made along the way seem to wall us in. We find, perhaps with horror or sadness, that we have painted ourselves in a corner by the paths we've chosen, the people we have loved, the promises we've made, and the unchosen circumstances and obligations of our lives. I have friends who feel stuck because they want to leave an ill-fitting job but cannot find other employment. Others who would like to move to a city where they have more friends but are the sole caretaker of an aging parent with a wasting disease. Others find their choices limited by the needs of a child with profound disabilities or a loved one with chronic mental illness. Some feel stuck because they and their spouse simply want different things and there's no clear compromise between the two.

I sat, not long ago, on my close friend Morgan's couch and told her that I felt stuck, cornered by commitments I'd made, unsure of how to go on. She didn't argue with me or suggest a clear next move, some easy escape plan. But she reminded me that, even if I did not see a way through, that did not mean that there was not one. God simply had not shown it to me yet. She reminded me that things can shift unexpectedly, not just in circumstances, but in our hearts. I may be stuck. God was not. My call, for now, was to wait and to persevere—to pledge my body to the walls.

Taking up stability is a way of getting ourselves stuck. That is the point.

The place of stuckness is not to be feared or fled. It may involve grief. But it is also the way of grace and inner transformation, the way of becoming, little by little, who we are meant to be. The Arabic word for patience comes from the same word as "to confine or contain."[6] This hints that patience is impossible to learn until we find ourselves confined—by our choices, our time, our relationships, our weaknesses, and our commitments. Though constraint is often looked at as oppressive or harmful in our culture, in reality, the confinements of our lives are the scaffolding required to learn to love abundantly, because love is patient. To stay in the cell is not to be imprisoned. It is not sheer drudgery or duty. The cell that confines us is the willing constraints of love.

III.

I have found that there is a way I flee my cell or abandon my nest without ever moving geographically—without, seemingly, making any changes at all.

In the midst of my spiritual midlife crisis, I would catch myself retracing my steps. I'd think nostalgically of a time in college, a time when I was full of zeal, the times long ago when God felt close. I looked back to all the places I'd lived and friends I once had. I looked back to when my kids were babies. I looked back at when the work I'd done was all excitement. And I fantasized about a different life. I fantasized about other jobs I had not taken, other places I had not lived, other men I had not married, other conversations I never had and wished I did, other lives I could have lived. I have a good imagination, one that's big enough for me to begin to live inside of it.

Fantasy is to imagine how life could be better, more whole, more complete "if only." If only I'd made better choices. If only I was more disciplined. If only I was more talented or organized. If only I had better friends. If only I had a nicer home, more money, or more time.

My fantasy life, of course, had no flaws in it, no awkwardness, no conflict, no uncertainty, no pimples or mosquitoes. But the lie offered to me by fantasy is not only that the perfection I imagine is not real. The lie is that what I really need is something other than for God to meet me in the moment I am in and in the life that I actually have. What fantasy offers is escape, not transformation.

The Orthodox writer Nicole Roccas argues that a mark of acedia—or, as she calls it, despondency—is an injured or disordered relationship with time.[7] We do not or cannot stay in our moment, in the minute we are in. On the widescreens of our hearts, we project images of what our life may have been or could be or will be, if only. Caught in the riptide of fantasy, we are dragged away from our present tense. This slowly engenders in us a hatred for what is present—our place, people, institutions, and obligations.

Acedia is often referred to as the "noonday demon" because it assails the monk midday, when the sun is highest and seems to stand still, when time itself seems to drag.[8] But evoking midday seems appropriate for this spiritual struggle in the course of a life, as well. It typically finds us not in the bright morning of joy and energy, nor in the dark horror of night, but in the long middle. Here, the temptation to fantasy is acute.[9] We realize that each choice along the way has brought us to today—and for most of us, if we're honest, there are things we enjoy about that and things we don't. But those places of regret, those places where we kick against the pricks of time, are, in the hands of God, where all the treasure is buried.

We must accept the circumstances of today—perhaps especially those we wouldn't have chosen—as the place of our formation. Staying in our cell is to meet God not in how our life could be or should be but in what it actually is, today, in this moment. Grace finds us, only ever, in the present tense.

IV.

A few years ago, a popular writer posted something online about how "true artists," those *really* committed to the craft, must flee from the interruptions and pressures of life and abscond to the woods to write in deepest, unbroken concentration for a week. My friends who were both artists and mothers passed around his words, guffawing. If we waited for the wooded cabin, we would never create a thing, they laughed. And they swapped stories about watching their child's fingers slip pleadingly under their studio doors, or balancing their laptop on their legs during a kid's track meet. They knew that, for them, the fantasy of the cabin in the woods was a trap. It would keep them from the work they needed to do today, amid the various and complex vocations that they had in the life they actually lived. This is similarly true in the craft of faith.

The truth is, my life is nothing like a monk's. I wake up each day, not to chimes calling my community to prayer, but to the dog scratching at his crate, or to voices of children calling for breakfast or fighting over who gets the bathroom first. I do not live, like Amma Syncletica, in a vast desert but in a bustling city with airplanes droning overhead and wifi in every shop.

The stories of saints and monks of old are a guide and a tutor, but for me, they can also breed a species of temptation that I have come to call the monastic fantasy.

Each year I read from *The Genesee Diary*, Henri Nouwen's chronicle of the seven months he spent in a Benedictine monastery. He writes about slow, daily rhythms of community, manual work, prayer, and quiet study. He embraced a life of order, self-discovery, and seemingly endless reams of time. As I read it during the pandemic, stuck inside a small house with relentless Zoom meetings and lovely but loud children, I found myself feeling deeply, bitterly, longingly jealous.[10] I knew on some level that Nouwen and the monks of that community experienced conflicts, boredom, and bad moods. They did not float from spiritual bliss to spiritual bliss. But I indulged in a fantasy. I imagined a life devoid of struggle—the freedom, the solitude, the expansive times of prayer, the shared chores, the slow pace, and the quiet. Oh, the blessed freakin' quiet.

But Nouwen had spiritual fantasies, too, even in the monastery. He tells his spiritual director, the abbot, that he dreams about how someday God will mystically "reveal himself . . . in such an intensive and convincing way" that Nouwen will be free of sins that had so long dogged him, and that then he could commit himself unconditionally to God. In response, the abbot is neither surprised nor impressed. "You want God to appear to you in the way your passions desire," he says, "but these passions make you blind to his presence now."[11] He calls Nouwen—and me—to recall that we are not meant to live life grasping at an ideal, even a spiritual ideal. The life we have today is the only classroom where we can learn the craft of faith. And the only cell that I have is the chaos that is my actual kitchen table.

V.

There is another story of Antony in the sayings of the fathers and mothers. Once, when he was living in the Egyptian desert, "his soul was troubled by boredom and irritation"—an apt description of our own modern malaise.

He asked God to cure him of this and make him whole. After a while, the story goes, he got up and went outside his cave. There, in the middle of nowhere, "he saw someone like himself sitting down and working, then standing up to pray; then sitting down again to make a plait of palm leaves, and standing up again to pray." In other words, the exact same things Antony did in his cell each day. This was said to be "an angel of the Lord sent to correct Antony and make him vigilant." The angel said, "Do this and you will be cured." When he heard it, Antony was "very glad and recovered his confidence."[12]

It's a weird story. Antony receives a vision from God, but there is no shaft of light, no choirs of singing angels, no call to some dangerous mission. God rends the heavens to reveal an average Tuesday.

In this vision, Antony saw himself continuing in his way and rule of life: praying, working, standing up, sitting down, rinse, repeat. It would be like God opening the clouds to reveal a vision of you just going to work, praying your prayers, crawling through traffic, making dinner, brushing your teeth, and tracking your family budget. Glory! Hallelujah!

The cure we are looking for, when we are bored or irritated with life, is rarely found in an escape, an ideal, or some dramatic spiritual breakthrough. It is not found in fleeing the cell or leaving the nest. It is found in developing the resilience it takes to keep going—to stay at the craft of faith and the work we have been given, in the place where we dwell, with the people around us. Antony's cure was found simply in persevering in small, faithful ways.

The things of God, it turns out, are surprisingly prosaic, ordinary, and unimpressive. If salvation is to meet us at all, it must meet us in the slog. We pray. We wait. We are patient. We persevere. And God rends the heavens to meet us in the last place that we expect to find him: exactly where we are.

4

Wait in the Womb

how hope transforms perseverance and fosters resilience

I.

Taylor Swift's hit 2024 song "I Can Do It with a Broken Heart" is upbeat, boppy, thoroughly danceable, and utterly depressing.[1]

She wrote it about the experience of managing a breakneck touring schedule while grieving the end of a long-term romantic relationship. Swift's personal world was falling apart, but she continued to perform each night before exuberant, record-breaking crowds on her Eras Tour. She gave herself to her craft, regardless of her feelings.

The song is part defiance, part lament, and presumably part critique. "They said, 'Babe, you gotta fake it till you make it,' and I did," she sings over a frenetic beat that mimics the pace of a person trying to outrun pain. She tells herself to "smile, even when you want to die." And she says that you know you are really good when you can do it all with a broken heart. The song ends with her confessing that she's "miserable, and nobody even knows!"

The author Ryan Holiday cites this song as a contemporary summary of Stoicism, an ancient philosophy that is currently making a comeback in popular culture. "You keep going," Holiday explains. "You do your best. Even if life has kicked the crap out of you. Even if someone has twisted your insides up. Even if you're depressed. Even if you're anxious. Even if you're tired, so tired. Even if nobody knows. Even if nobody understands. You've got a job to do, a duty to fulfill."[2]

That could sure sound a little like "stay in your cell." And if Stoicism is the lens through which we see this call, it may seem as if I'm saying that Christian faithfulness requires one to be miserable in work, church, marriage, friendships, and faith, and to just keep going. Never fall apart. Never grieve. Never stop. And if you're doing it right, no one will even know how miserable you are.

But this is decidedly not what stability or staying in your cell means. This is critical to understand: It does not matter simply that we "stay in our cell." It matters why and how we do so.

When monastic hermits embrace utter solitude and silence, they report finding peace, growth, even miraculous encounters with God. And prisoners in solitary confinement, found similarly alone in silence, can be driven mad by it. It's the same practice, in some sense, but an utterly different experience.

The why and the how changes the practice. The why and how changes everything.

Certainly, fragments of Stoicism are found nearly everywhere in Western culture, including in the hearts of many a churchgoer. If you, like me, grew up in a home that embraced grit and hard work, you're likely familiar with the idea that in the face of pain, we just need to "suck it up" and keep trucking. But this approach to life leaves us cynical and depleted, embroiled in hidden pain or failure, ashamed of our vulnerability, disconnected from God and other people. Willpower and dogged impassivity do not form us into people capable of Christian faithfulness. Many have kept at their duty, stayed in their cell, and ended up bitter, joyless, and resentful.

Early Christians saw much to admire in Stoicism's emphasis on perseverance, patience, and fortitude, but they also recognized a pivotal difference in the Christian understanding of these virtues—a difference that utterly transforms our experience of them. And that difference is hope.

Many ancient Stoic philosophers believed that at the end of history there would be a giant conflagration. Everything in the universe would be destroyed and reborn—and this cycle would repeat and replay itself eternally, with no hope for change.[3] In this understanding of the world, there is no knowable, loving God who makes all things new. Instead, life is tragedy, and we are on our own. No one is coming to rescue us. Our lives, our destinies, our society, and our flourishing are therefore all up to us. It's all on our shoulders. So we just keep going. This may make us dutiful, but it cannot marry duty with delight.

For Christians, the story that shapes the why and the how of everything—the story that forms our practices and motivations—is the story of Jesus bringing us into the very life of the Trinity. This hope transforms the practice of perseverance. It turns mere endurance into expectation.

Christian perseverance does not ask us to grit our teeth through life. Instead, we learn to wait expectantly for Jesus's continuing story of redemption to unfold, in every part of the planet and in our own days and weeks and years. We keep at our commitments—we stay in our cell—not because we have no choice other than doing it all with a broken heart, but because we are learning to wait on a God who loves us, who sees our broken hearts, and who (often slowly, sometimes painfully) brings repair and healing.

The cells of our lives, then, are not merely places of persistence and steadfastness, but places of encounter and transformation. This is how the Desert Mothers and Fathers understood the call to stay in the cell.

One Desert Father compared the monk's cell to "the furnace in Babylon where the three young men found the Son of God."[4] In the book of Daniel, Shadrach, Meshach, and Abednego are thrown into a furnace to be brutally killed because they've refused, against their king's demands, to worship a false god. The furnace, a place of death, becomes instead the site of a miracle. Not only are the young men unharmed, but there is a fourth man walking among the flames. The king says this man "looks like a son of the gods."[5]

In the furnace, these young men found not just rescue, but God himself. The miracle of the furnace is not the three young men's internal composure or steadfast faith. The miracle is that God himself showed up when everything seemed past hope.

The miracle is *God with us.*

We stay in the cell because God himself is waiting there, in the furnace and the desert—in the distress and disorientation, of our lives, our work, our relationships, our questions, and our commitments. The cell becomes the site of theophany.

II.

C. S. Lewis corresponded with an American woman who was struggling with doubt and worried that God found her a hopeless case. Whatever she might be feeling about God or herself on a given day, Lewis encouraged her to "continue seeking with cheerful seriousness," knowing that unless God "wanted you, you would not be wanting Him."[6]

I've come to think that this phrase "cheerful seriousness" is what it looks like to be a resilient people. This is who the church is meant to be.

We are a serious people. We do not pretend that the darkness is any less dark than it truly is. We do not presume that with enough money, technology, fame, or power, we could avoid trouble, death, persecution, or pain. We do not act as if the problems in the world or our own lives are easy to solve. We take our relationships with our neighbors and with God seriously.

And yet, as Jesus told his disciples to be, we remain, intentionally and authentically, "of good cheer." The reason Jesus gave his followers for remaining cheerful was not a promise that if they did their duty, all things would go their way or that they would not grow weary. Instead, he promises that "in the world you will have tribulation," yet we can rest in knowing that he has "overcome the world."[7] The hope that Jesus has overcome the world is what orients our perseverance. It is what fuels our resilience.

In my last book, I grappled with theodicy: the question of how God can be good and all-knowing when bad things regularly happen in the world. At first, I did not want to write it. I told God in prayer that if I wrote a book about suffering and grief, readers would approach me at book signings, in letters, and at conferences, to tell me the worst things that had ever happened to them. "I can't take it," I said. "I'll hear of all the most painful things in people's lives, and I'll despair. My faith will falter. I'll lose hope."

I ended up writing the book anyway because, like a stray cat that follows you home, it wouldn't leave me alone. And turns out, I was right.

After it was published, I heard hundreds, if not thousands, of stories of pain, of trauma, of grief and loss. I heard stories of pediatric cancer, of mental illness, of deep betrayal, of people reading my words from a dreary hospital room feeling shattered and lost. It was—it is—heartbreaking. The darkness only seems darker now. But something else happened that I had not predicted.

Readers would tell me about the worst things that had happened in their lives, but the story wouldn't stop there.

They would keep talking. They would describe to me how God had met them in their agony. They would tell me about slow and painful healing, about redemption, about how light had come in the darkness. And there they were: still standing, still breathing, still believing, testifying through tears that there is a deeper goodness at work in the world than I had thought possible. They had faced the worst. Yet they told me, in a thousand different ways, that Jesus has overcome the world. It always feels like a miracle to me.

It's not that they were now okay or happy with the loss or trauma they had met. It was still the worst thing to ever happen to them. But there was more. They had hope. And their stories have slowly taught me to hope.

This is what the church is meant to be: the place where we can honestly talk about the worst things that have happened to us, the worst things that have happened in the world, and even just the worst things to happen in our ordinary week, and together proclaim a greater and enduring hope. This hope is, of course, most embodied in our Communion meal of bread and wine. A meal that reminds us of the very worst thing, a meal of death, humiliation, and defeat that mysteriously becomes the very presence of God to us. Each time we show up to church, we come bearing our broken hearts with other brokenhearted people, to the God who was broken and who promises to mend us and all things.

This meal makes clear that hope is not optimism, naïveté, or perkiness. Christian hope does not belong to "bright prospects and the morning," G. K. Chesterton writes, those moments when we feel confident and at ease. It's not the same as focusing on the bright side or wishing for the best. It is when things feel intractable, like nothing can get better, that hope begins to matter. "Exactly at the instant when hope ceases to be reasonable it begins to be useful," says Chesterton.[8]

True hope is not born from our good decisions, well-ordered homes and families, or exciting or adventurous lives. It cannot be bought, curated, or posted. Instead, true hope is born when the dream of what we thought life would be begins to fall apart and die. It is found when we are most tempted to despair, when any ability to hold our lives together through our gifts or strength goes up in flames, and at last, we begin to wait on God for rescue.

Hope is what allows lament. It is what allows us the emotional honesty to rage at the heavens, yet collapse into the hands of a loving God.

Paul wrote to the church in Rome that "suffering produces endurance" (or perseverance or "patient continuance"), "endurance produces character, and character produces hope."[9] These verses have been called an "ascending chain," with each virtue giving rise to the one that follows.[10] Perseverance produces "character," a word Paul uses to mean, essentially, "tested" and "proven."

Think of metal being proven. This can mean various things. It can mean testing its purity, ensuring, for instance, that a gold ring is actually fourteen karats. It can mean identifying its chemical composition, the stuff it is made of. Or it can mean determining its strength and ability to withstand stress or force. Paul suggests that this is what persevering amid struggle does in us. It proves us and purifies us. It clarifies what we are made of and reveals our strength so we can become who we are made to be and do what we are meant to do.

This proven character yields hope. In this ascending chain, it is struggle and difficulty, not ease or success, that lead to hope. This understanding of reality is profoundly countercultural and perhaps counterintuitive for us. Our tendency, quite naturally, is to shrink back from pain, to seek to rid our lives of difficulty whenever possible. Our assumption can be that suffering leaves us weaker and more fragile—this is particularly clear in how we often speak about the irreversible harm caused by traumatic experiences. While the scriptures certainly do not make light of traumatic events, they also do not see them as an unbreachable barrier to human flourishing. Hope is born from the worst of circumstances. "Just as resistance to a muscle strengthens it," writes the New Testament scholar Douglas Moo, "so challenges to our hope can strengthen it."[11]

God, despite how he has been portrayed at times, does not gleefully inflict human suffering to teach us some Sunday school lesson or prove some theological point. But God also wastes nothing in our lives. Suffering can, in the hands of God, become an ascent—a way that we learn to persevere, a way that we are proven, a way that we take up hope, which Chesterton defines as "the power of being cheerful in circumstances which we know to be desperate."[12]

Resistance to hope—spirits of cynicism and despair—is all

around us in our culture, in politics, in violence, in the headlines, and in the dark corners of our hearts. But for the Christian, this resistance is the very place where training in hope begins. It is the struggle that tills us, that breaks us open, so that hope can be planted and take root.

III.

If hope is to grow in us, it will be sown and nourished together, in community with other people. Particularly when we are tired, we cannot take up hope on our own. We need, as the book of Galatians points out, others who will bear our burdens with us.[13]

As Christians, we learn to hope through the beauty and frailty of a local congregation, a community of real people right around us, who doubt and believe, who delight us or annoy us, who can pray for us and wrestle with questions right along with us.

This means, practically, that we show up to church, but more than that, that we show who we truly are to our church. We tell trusted friends about our struggles and doubts. We ask for help. We do not hide.

Hope does not grow by pretending. If we are "miserable and nobody even knows," we are being dishonest with those we need the most. We've cut ourselves off from the very place where hope can germinate.

In an interview with me for *The New York Times,* the writer and psychiatrist Curt Thompson linked our ability to heal from burnout with our ability to connect with other people who love us. "We know that the brain can do a lot of really hard things for a long time, as long as it doesn't have to do them by itself," Thompson said. "We only develop greater resilience when we are deeply emotionally connected to other people."

The rhythms and habits of our society—everything from how cities are designed to how we raise our children to how most of us spend an average weekend—make connection with others more difficult. Thompson told me that, as a culture, "we have been practicing isolation for much longer than we know. We build it into our daily routines. We build it into our social media behavior. We have practiced liturgies of isolationism."

If our culture forms us in liturgies of isolation, we need counterpractices of connection and community. Thompson's advice is to "pick one person, pick two people, and say . . . 'I would like to begin to meet with you once a week and just talk about where we are, talk about our stories. Let's talk about what's been hard, and not try to fix things but to be present with each other.' "[14]

This does not mean, of course, that we share our sorrows, shame, or struggles with anyone and everyone. But it means that we have to call the friend, even when it feels vulnerable to do so. We have to ask the pastor out for coffee. We have to show up at church, and when someone there asks how the week has been, not just mutter "fine." We have to look someone in the eyes and be honest about who we are and where we are. We have to tell our secrets.

IV.

Amma Syncletica compared our whole lives and everything in them to "a second maternal womb." In the womb, she said, "we did not have there solid nourishment such as we enjoy now, nor were we able to be active, indeed, as we are here, and we in fact existed without the light of the sun and of any glimmer of light . . . so also in the present world we are impoverished in comparison with the kingdom of heaven."[15] The womb is not a place of grim endurance. Time in the womb is never wasted or meaningless. The womb is a place of mystery, formation, and growth. It is a place of beauty and purpose yet a place of waiting for something more.

Amma Syncletica implies we are the baby, waiting unaware, not the parent. But in my own life, the metaphor resonates as a mother. I recall that each time I have carried a baby, I always felt a lot of disorientation and uncertainty. With each pregnancy, I'd go for days and weeks looking for any sign that something was happening, any hint that a human being was developing in my body. I'd thump my slowly growing belly with my thumb, trying to get my baby to thump back. I wanted signs of life. A nudge. A kick. A hiccup. A roll. I'd take anything.

And now, in this desert season, I do the same with God. I thump the heavens, waiting for a response, a nudge—or a kick—waiting for a reminder that times of silence do not mean I am alone. I'm on the watch for a sign that something is growing and forming imperceptibly in me.

The metaphor of our whole life being like a womb beautifully manages to honor the goodness and importance of our lives here and now while also orienting them toward a future hope, a world where God has set all things right. "We have sampled the nourishment here," Syncletica says, "let us reach for the divine! We have enjoyed the light in this world; let us long for the sun of righteousness!"[16] Her words are perhaps deeper than she could have known, given all that we now know about embryology and how development in the womb affects who we are outside of it. We know, of course, that a pregnant woman drinking a fifth of vodka each day can have long-term effects on a child his whole life, just as we know that singing or talking to a baby in the womb teaches her to recognize her mother's and father's voices outside of it. In the same way, our formation in this world, today, even this minute, is a continuing part of who we will be eternally. The most striking thing to me about Syncletica's metaphor is the fundamental *continuity* between now and what is to come.

Our lives, our choices, and our actions today matter because we are being formed for a birth; we are heading toward something solid, lasting, and more real than we now know. But at moments, even now, we hear hints of the world outside this womb, a voice of love that we are just beginning to place, a faraway song whose rhythm we are just starting to learn. These beckon us from outside this world.

In this way, the Christian faith is not meant to quench our sense of longing, but to heighten it and to direct it toward its intended end. It is not meant to make our desires smaller, our hunger sated, our yearning silenced, but to draw us into their depths that we might learn how they are met only in our Maker.

In a sermon titled "The Weight of Glory," C. S. Lewis discusses "the inconsolable secret" in each one of us, "the secret which hurts so much that you take your revenge on it by calling it names like Nostalgia and Romanticism and Adolescence; the secret also which pierces with such sweetness that when, in very intimate conversation, the mention of it becomes imminent, we grow awkward and affect to laugh at ourselves; the secret we cannot hide and cannot tell, though we desire to do both." He says that we cannot tell of this deep secret—our wild sense of longing—because it is birthed from a desire "for something that has never actually appeared in our experience," but "we cannot hide it because our experience is constantly suggesting it."[17]

The best things in this world point to something greater, something better than anything we have ever actually found. It is good and right to enjoy the things of this world—the nourishment and light to be found here. We ought to enjoy the scent of coffee beans or the feel of cool water on a hot day or laughing with a friend. But each good thing is a foretaste intended to whet our appetite for our true life—in Syncletica's metaphor, our life after birth.

Christian hope is born from the belief that the very best things in heaven and earth will not pass away into fire or emptiness, but will be made more solid, lasting, and real—not in some far-off heaven, but in the renewal and resurrection of this beloved world.

In moments of deep beauty or simply in the quiet corners of our day, longing wells up. On winter nights when firelight dapples the living room, in the swelling of a symphony, or when my congregation sings in harmony on Christmas Eve, I feel a warm ache, a weighty emptiness. I yearn for beauty that lasts.

To get by in a weary world, we numb out. We try to squelch our sense of longing, to make it smaller and flatter, to dull its ache with television, good takeout, work success, or whatever small dopamine release we can find easily at hand. We deny our deepest yearnings and tell ourselves to be practical, to grow up, to leave behind desire for something more and learn to live with disappointment. But some honest, human part of us yet remains that knows a longing we just can't shake.

We flame out when we try to quench this longing in our own

way on our own timeline, when we seek to eke out happiness and fulfillment by our own determination, best thinking, and control. We try to satiate our longing here and now.

But we go deep by following our longing as an explorer follows a river to the great, wide sea. Both the source and the end of longing—our "inconsolable secret"—is our Maker. We wait in the womb of our lives, for the day when our deepest longings will be fulfilled in the only way they can be.

My whole life is a womb. And whatever I feel at the moment—whether or not it seems anything much is happening—I am being formed for something more. We wait in hope to be brought, blinking, beloved, wide awake, into the light of day. The end is an arrival.

5

Relax the Bow

how grace transforms our efforts

I.

If there was an award for the most calligraphed verse of all time, "Be still and know that I am God" would probably win it. Even if you've never darkened the door of a church, you've likely seen this statement from Psalm 46. It is splashed around Etsy shops, displayed in cursive on shiplapped walls, and inked on wrists, forearms, or ankles.

I suspect the phrase is so marketable because we all frequently feel frantic, hurried, and hustling. A call to stillness is a welcome balm to weary and worried souls. But the ubiquity of this verse can strip it of its meaning. I've seen it, at times, rendered simply, "Be still and know." Shorn of any theological context, it is unclear what, exactly, we are supposed to "know." It may seem like a call to "trust yourself and your intuition" or something equally vague—some ambiguous spiritual feeling, some inarticulable "knowing." The part of this verse that is quoted widely, however, is just a snippet. The verse keeps going: "Be still, and know that I am God: I will be exalted among the nations, I will be exalted in the earth."[1]

Stillness, in the mind of the Psalmist, does not arise from finding a calm morning after a long week, or from a shapeless "knowing" that we find inside ourselves. The Psalmist is called by God to be still because God—not me, not you, not us—is God, and he will be exalted in every square inch of human existence. It is God, the Psalmist writes, who makes wars to cease, who shatters weapons, melts spears, and brings mercy, justice, and beauty.

This word translated "be still" in Hebrew more literally means to slacken, to loosen, to relax, to unclench our hands and let go. It is sometimes translated as "stop striving,"[2] and this particular translation always gets my attention because the root cause of my lack of stillness—the cause of my disquiet and anxiety—is not just that I have a full and busy life. There's a lie ensconced in the corner of my heart—a lie that our culture enshrines as truth. It whispers that it is up to me to hold my life together through my hard work, through my accomplishments, through measuring up, through having the right body and brain and soul. It tells me that I must never stop striving.

But this Psalm reminds us that God isn't holding his breath, anxious that we get it all right so that things can work out for us and for the world (and for him). We can be still because we have a deep-down confidence that, when all is said and done, God wins. This reality does not only offer us a future hope. It also changes the rhythm and tenor of the here and now. It transforms what it looks and feels like to stay in the cell.

II.

It is not hard to see that the Desert Fathers and Mothers were wholehearted in their commitment to God. They lived with levels of discipline and austerity that make the most intense ascetic today seem like a bit of a wimp. And certainly, there are times when I think they go overboard with this. I was once in my neighborhood bakery, savoring their fancy gourmet coffee, while reading the Desert Father Abba Poemen say that a "true monk" hates all "bodily comfort."[3] And I kept right on sipping my latte.

It may be easy to think of the fathers and mothers as inveterate strivers, who simply exchanged our usual drives for wealth, fame, or success for a quest for salvation. In the midst of their rigor and discipline, however, there are moments when I suddenly find a beautiful sense of lightheartedness, restfulness, and gentleness in their practice of faith. I find grace.

These men and women did not feel that the life of faith rested all on their shoulders. They saw their efforts as a response to God's work and mercy—as a way to be free from the entanglements of the world so that they could pursue true life and real joy. They described all their efforts as "little" and "small."[4] They understood that they were sinful and limited, and constantly reiterated the need to not judge others.

They sought God with cheerful seriousness. They were wholehearted, yet lighthearted.

Take this story of Saint Antony for example. One day, the story goes, a hunter happened upon Antony "talking in a relaxed way with the brothers." The hunter was shocked to see the revered saint just hanging out, taking it easy. Antony noticed the hunter's surprise and said to him, "Put an arrow in your bow, and draw it." He did so. Then Antony said, "Draw it further," and he drew it further. He said, "Draw it yet further," and the hunter drew it some more. Finally, the hunter objected. "If I draw it too far, the bow will snap." Antony answered, "So it is with God's work. If we always go to excess, the brothers quickly become exhausted. It is sometimes best not to be rigid."[5]

Antony, who regularly fasted and prayed, who intentionally lived in poverty and took up long stretches of solitude, also clearly understood the need for gentleness. He saw that slacking off can be a holy endeavor. This gentle discipline—wholeheartedness yet lightheartedness—is key to understanding our call to perseverance and resilience.

Another little line from Abba Poemen reflects this lighthearted flexibility in the craft of faith. Poemen was asked how he dealt with fellow monks who fell asleep during public prayer. He didn't shame or judge or lecture them. He didn't tell a weary monk to try harder or be stronger. Instead, he answered, "I put his head upon my knees and help him to rest."[6]

One day when everything—writing, mothering, marriage, preaching, praying, getting out of bed—felt particularly difficult, I came upon advice from the memoirist Mary Karr: "As writing gets harder, go at it softer," she wrote. "The instinct to attack harder comes from fear. But that just pours animal energy into the scared place. Move slower. Take more breaks. Breathe deeper. Honor your insides. Notice stuff. Celebrate doing it at all."[7]

It felt like a kind word from a friend. It felt like Antony and Poemen's gentleness. And it applies not just to writing but to prayer and believing, to friendship or parenting, to all of life.

The story of Jesus tells us that we ought not stay in our cell with anxiety sketched on our face, as if our lives are in our clenched hands. We can let go. Loosen our grip. Be still. Because God, in Christ, has won and will win, we can continue in work and prayer, but without a sense of panic or perfectionism.

So instead of being disappointed in myself for not waking up at six A.M. for an hour of silence, maybe I could wake up at seven A.M. and pray for ten minutes a couple times a day. If attempting deep, concentrated, creative work for four hours feels like a pointless experiment in medieval torture, maybe I could try two hours and a short walk. When I grumpily snapped at my five-year-old, I could try not to spend the rest of the day imagining his future breakthrough memoir, *How My Sorry Excuse for a Mother Ruined My Life.* Instead, I could apologize, accept his abundant five-year-old grace, and try again with mercy toward myself and others.

What matters most is not some imagined heroics—some sense of what we should be—but instead the small work, the thousands and thousands of attempts, confusion, failure, learning, and growing. Perfectionism tells us that anything done poorly is not worth doing, but this fearful striving ultimately keeps us from growth.

Fear of screwing up—of doing it poorly—is what, in the parable of the talents in Matthew's Gospel, keeps a worker from investing his talent.[8] In the parable, a master gives three servants talents, which is a large sum of money. Two invest the money and make a profit. But one buries it, and later explains to his boss, the "master," that he was afraid because he knew him to be "a hard man." This third worker is scared of messing up, of getting a bad grade on the assignment, of incurring anger. It's not that the two other workers are so much smarter at business. It's not that they're perfect people with perfect teeth and perfect hearts and beachwave hair. It's that they trust the character of the one who has entrusted his wealth to them. They do not believe they have a hard master. And because of that trust and that risk, they end up experiencing astonishing returns.

So we stay at our small attempts at love, prayer, and work knowing they may often be faltering or frustrating. We hold to the hope that it is mercy, not our accomplishments, discipline, or striving that brings the harvest, the reward, the return. And, in everything—as Karr said—we celebrate doing it at all. We honor the small victories of the one decent paragraph we got written, or the brief, happy conversation with a co-worker or spouse, or the ten minutes of solitude we found in an overly busy day.

God does not roll his eyes, waiting for us to muscle up and prove our worth. It is only when we know that God is gentle with us that we can risk doing it all badly and see what God, in time, makes of our feeble efforts.

III.

Believing that God is gentle with us allows us to, in the words of the writer Martin Shaw, make a "covenant with limit," to honor our weaknesses and finitude.[9] Thomas Merton quotes an unnamed Desert Father saying, "The reason why we do not get anywhere is that we do not know our limits."[10] There is something in the psyche of us strivers that feels ashamed of having limits. We want to keep our edge, to not age or grow tired, to not let our cracks show. We tell ourselves that we should be able to handle it all, that we ought not need help or rest. But to gain resilience in the face of weariness, we must learn how to let go, to bend the bow but not break it.

I have a friend and mentor, Mary, who got ordained in the early eighties when relatively few women wore a collar. Mary is a groundbreaker and a force—smart, assertive, a leader by nature, with a sharp wit and easy smile. I met her soon after I was ordained, and I found her inspiring and also a little intimidating. Now semi-retired, for much of her life she worked full-time as a pastor and was a national leader in her denomination, addressing complex problems and conflicts, all while raising her kids and making time to encourage younger priests like me.

When people ask her, "How did you do it all?," her usual reply is: "I regularly fell apart." When I first heard her answer, it disarmed me; I started laughing. Mary seems so together, so strong, so capable. But she is also honest.

She told me that regularly—maybe every few months or so—she'd hit a wall. The physical and emotional toll of her work, her family, her church, and relationships would leave her depleted. And because she was strong and wise, she let herself fall apart. "I'd stay in my bathrobe all day," she told me. She'd sleep or read a magazine or journal or stare at the ceiling. She'd come downstairs for a minute just to make sure her kids and husband were still alive, then right back upstairs to fall apart some more. She tells people about this—especially younger people—because it gives other people permission to do the same. She wants others to know that there is no shame in hitting your limit and stopping. She wants people to know that their limits are from God and should be honored and embraced, not resisted. After a day or so of falling apart, she said, she would feel like she could keep going. And she did, for decades.

There are seasons when we can't fall apart for the whole day. Other people are depending on us. But maybe we can fall apart for an afternoon or for a couple of hours. It takes trust to let go, to cease striving. It takes trust to believe that we don't have to scissors-hold our life together with willpower, energy, calendaring, and duct tape. We don't have a hard master. We can fall apart and trust God to put our head upon his knees and help us rest.

IV.

If we stay in our cell, there will undoubtedly be times when we blow it. I do not mean that we will fall apart, get weary, and meet with our natural limitations.

I mean that we will fail. There will be times when we don't pray, not so much because we are simply exhausted, but because we are steeped in resentful or jealous thoughts about our enemies. There will be times when we don't rise to the demands of our work because we have collapsed into acedia, spending hours watching Instagram reels. There will be times we do not respond to the needs of the people entrusted to us, not out of weariness but because we are unforgiving or impatient or mean or self-righteous. And, maybe in those moments, just for a second, we see ourselves with a new kind of honesty. We catch a glimpse of something shameful in our soul, like a shoplifter caught on a hidden camera.

This is part of what our cell has to teach us. If we stay at Christian practices, in a community, and in commitments long enough, we will inevitably come to see deep patterns of brokenness and sin in our lives. This is a necessary, though profoundly uncomfortable, part of going deep.

One of my favorite stories from the sayings of the Desert Fathers and Mothers is about a monk who blew it:

> A brother fell when he was tempted, and in his distress he stopped practising his monastic rule. He really longed to take it up again, but his own misery prevented him. He

> would say to himself, "When shall I be able to be holy in the way I used to be before?"
>
> He went to see one of the old men, and told him all about himself. And when the old man learned of his distress, he said: "There was a man who had a plot of land; but it got neglected and turned into waste ground, full of weeds and brambles. So he said to his son, 'Go and weed the ground.' The son went off to weed it, saw all the brambles and despaired. He said to himself, 'How long will it take before I have uprooted and reclaimed all that?' So he lay down and went to sleep for several days. His father came to see how he was getting on and found he had done nothing at all. 'Why have you done nothing?' he said. The son replied, 'Father, when I started to look at this and saw how many weeds and brambles there were, I was so depressed that I could do nothing but lie down on the ground.' His father said, 'Child, just go over the surface of the plot every day and you will make some progress.' So he did, and before long the whole plot was weeded. The same is true for you, brother: work just a little bit without getting discouraged, and God by his grace will re-establish you."[11]

It's such a relatable story. I have certainly looked at the mess in the world and in my own life—how much is awry, how much needs to change, how many weeds and brambles are growing wild in my heart—and felt that all I could do was lie down and sleep for several days. But the father's response in the story is both patient and practical. He offers the possibility of grace and the possibility of change, of repentance, of coming into more flourishing than we now feel is possible.

The story reminds us to not waste a minute of life thinking about how much better, more faithful, or more ardent we used to be. It also tells us that we won't get far trying to weed out the intractable sins in our lives or in the world all at once. To think we could is the kind of pride that leads to despair. The Spirit of God typically weeds us and restores us, little by little, day in and day out. It's slow work.

Each week in my church's liturgy, every one of us, from the priests to the preschoolers, gets on our knees and confesses that we have blown it—we've sinned against God and against others. It's the time when I feel the most solidarity with everyone around me.

Then there comes the part of the service called "the comfortable words." I've always loved this strange term. There are so many uncomfortable words—disordered, spiteful, manipulative, and merciless words—uttered all around us and inside of us each week. So together, as a church, we make room for words of comfort.

The priest reminds us that God is faithful to forgive, that there is nothing beyond the reach of God's mercy. And then he or she prays that God would "strengthen us in all goodness." This church, these friends and I who kneel beside one another each week, is the plot of earth, full of weeds, messy, overgrown, and disheveled, that God still works in and calls his own. Grace offers us forgiveness. And grace grows new shoots of goodness in us.

This saying from the Desert Fathers and Mothers does not tell us to keep working because our plot of land is in our hands and reliant on our efforts. Instead, the story reminds us that we can work, without discouragement, because it is God's grace, in the end, that reestablishes us. Day by day, bit by bit.

V.

Dorothy Day was a twentieth-century Catholic convert who spent her life serving God and those around her, particularly the poor. She launched the Catholic Worker Movement and lived in a communal house with others, including people with severe mental illness and addictions, in New York City. She knew deep suffering and struggle. But when I read her memoir and essays, the overwhelming sense of her life is that she reveled in beauty and celebrated each small joy.

"As one gets older," she wrote later in life, "we are tempted to sadness, knowing life as it is here on earth, the suffering, the Cross." We confront this by taking up what she called "the duty of delight."[12] In the midst of an intense life of service to the vulnerable—a life that required a long obedience and a whole lot of staying in her cell—Day intentionally valued small, beautiful things: the light falling through a sunny window, the cadence of a Dostoevsky novel, the steam from hot coffee on a cold morning. To her, these were hints of resurrection. They were glimpses of the grace and kindness of God.

In my season of aridity, I felt rich in responsibilities and obligations, but poor in levity, laughter, wonder, and joy. Part of what languishing does in us is slowly dull our delight. Part of its cure, then, is to intentionally reacquaint ourselves with gladness.

My church holds "quiet days" during Advent and Lent, when around a dozen of us go to Betsy's house and someone whisks away all the children for a few hours. Betsy is a member of my church and a trained spiritual director. She is kind and gentle, and I get the sense that nothing anyone says could shock or offend her at this point in her life. She loves to bake, and if you sit in her living room, she will hand you good coffee and a soft blanket.

I sit in Betsy's house on our quiet days, after she's sent us off to be silent, alone. And I just cry. I cry because it feels like someone is taking care of me. Because my own mother is sick and slowly drifting away, and I need someone to mother me for a few hours, and God sent Betsy with her Ina Garten cookbook collection. I cry because I want to hear from God but haven't in a long time. I cry because life is complicated and complex, and Betsy makes room for me to sit silently in all that complication and complexity for a while—to sit in it with others and with a homemade pumpkin nut muffin and with a babysitter I didn't pay for, and no one asking me to do anything for them.

At the end of each quiet day, we all sit in a circle and take turns saying what we are thinking about. People share about their struggles, hopes, or the way a particular meditation on scripture struck them. After each person shares, everyone sits together in silence for a long time and eventually asks questions or tells us if they think God said anything to them about us, and then we pray for one another. It's called group spiritual direction.

During a Lenten quiet day last year, I told my fellow parishioners about my sense of weariness, about feeling burdened and uncertain. A few people offered encouraging words and commiseration. My husband spoke up from across the room, "Your life is hard and heavy now, and I know you aren't sure if anything is working. I know you have a ton you have to do. We are both busy and we don't have a lot of free time. But we have to remember to make room for the duty of delight."

Over the past years, I had slowly developed a habit of feeling guilty about giving time to small pleasures or about "wasting" time on fun. If I was taking up the "duty of delight," it meant I was not doing the dishes, working on a book, helping kids with homework, or returning email. Jonathan challenged me to intentionally add things I loved into my day or week, just for the sheer joy of it. If I had to, he said, add it to the planner or write it on a to-do list: Walk in the woods at a nearby greenbelt. Read a book for fun. Lie on the backyard hammock on a sunny day. Get a cupcake from our nearby bakery. Be completely alone for an afternoon. Notice the sunset and the first appearance of Venus, bright and low in the evening sky.

We have many responsibilities in this life, but among them we must recall that we also have the blessed responsibility to take up those things that make life ever so slightly gentler.

One practical way to make room for delight is to practice the Sabbath, to give up on work and productivity for a day each week to embrace rest, worship, and play. To be clear, I have consistently practiced a Sabbath for two decades now, so plainly it is not a silver bullet for burnout or aridity. The desert, after all, is an unavoidable stage in our lives.

Still, my weekly rhythm of turning off the computer each Saturday evening, and intentionally not shopping, working, or being on screens for a day, gave me one bounded period each week where I did not feel guilty for getting absolutely nothing done.

The practice is never perfect. Even on bright, lovely Sunday mornings, kids still bicker and sometimes slug each other, or dogs still puke on the carpet, or I suddenly realize we are out of toilet paper, or my husband, lost in a book, forgets the pizza in the oven until it's burnt to a crisp. Certainly, friends or family often have urgent or time-sensitive needs. Life is unpredictable and complex. Yet there are fleeting moments in my day of rest when quiet beauty wraps around me, when my kids' peals of laughter echo through the hall, when we're all lost in books and the pizza still comes out just right. This small weekly quest for delight—without guilt, without pressure, without to-do lists—might not make weariness magically disappear. But I suspect it helps keep my head above water. Slacking off for one day each week is a way to recall that I can be still because God, not me, is the mover and shaker of my life. It is a temporal practice of gentleness, of trying softer.

I have an old friend who kept a photo on her desk of a turtle basking in the sun, resplendent in chelonian bliss. Above it, she wrote, "Never feel guilty for doing those things that feed your soul." These small moments of gentleness offer mercy and grace that we can touch, taste, and feel. And they recall the great hope underneath each moment of our lives: the hope that beauty will indeed save the world, that God, by his grace, will finally reestablish us and all things. Creation speaks its comfortable words over us.

6

Let the Silt Settle

silence and connecting to the Source

I.

In the sayings of the Desert Fathers and Mothers, there's another strange story. There were three friends who were monks, all earnest and faithful. One of them, motivated by the call in Matthew's Gospel to be a peacemaker, chose to spend his time seeking to "make peace between men who were at odds." The second monk, motivated by Christ's concern for the vulnerable, decided to "visit the sick." The third chose to "go away to be quiet in solitude."

The first monk did some good helping others to reconcile, but he grew sad over conflicts he could not solve. He felt "overcome with weariness." So he went to visit his friend who was tending the sick, only to discover that his friend, too, was "flailing in spirit."

The two men visited the third monk and told him about their exhaustion and sense of futility—what today we might call burnout.

The third monk sat silently for a long while, then he poured water into a cup. "Look at this water," he said. The water was murky with silt. But after they sat together for a while, the water settled. "See now, how clear the water has become," said the third monk. "So it is with anyone who lives in a crowd; because of the turbulence, he does not see his sins: but when he has been quiet, above all in solitude, then he recognizes his own faults."[1]

Each time I read this story, I want to argue with it. Don't some of us have to live in crowds? Doesn't *someone* have to make peace? Doesn't *someone* have to visit the sick?

Yet that's exactly what intrigues me about this story: how countercultural and counterintuitive it is to me. The first and second monks are motivated by such good and virtuous things. Their work is urgent and important. If this parable were told today, they would be the clear moral heroes, pouring themselves out in service to others. Yet despite their passion, or maybe because of it, they find themselves overcome by weariness and discouragement. Their solitary friend implies that they've lost perspective. They cannot see themselves, their faults, or their limitations clearly. What they need is withdrawal and quiet.

In college, I became unlikely friends with a chain-smoking Franciscan priest. Like all Franciscans, he'd taken a vow of poverty. He was brilliant and kind, and I could not doubt his commitment to the marginalized. Soon after graduation, I bumped into the friar, and we caught up. I told him about my job running a church-based program for recent immigrants, which provided tutoring and ESL classes for kids and help for families in poverty. It was beautiful and rewarding work, but also intense, difficult, and draining. A few minutes into our conversation, he looked at me with compassion and said matter-of-factly, "You don't have the life of prayer and silence necessary to sustain the work you are doing."

I was taken aback. *What does he know?* I thought. I was zealous and passionate about seeking justice and helping others—perhaps a little like the first two monks. My friend was not telling me to quit my job, but he was calling me to learn to be more like the third. And, in the end, he was right. Within a couple of years, I was burned out and discouraged. I had been all energy and fire, but I simply did not have the practices of prayer and solitude necessary to cultivate the wisdom, humility, and stability of heart that my life and work demanded.[2]

The desert monks tended to value withdrawal obsessively. One would have to in order to leave civilization and survive as a hermit for decades.[3] Though the Desert Fathers and Mothers universally insist that we must respond materially when someone sick or in need crosses our path, at times their writings seem to elevate solitude and withdrawal as being more spiritually important than participation in the workaday world.

In contrast, our culture tends to be equally obsessive in the opposite direction. We overvalue work, accolades, output, and applause. We live in and among the crowd, nearly constantly. Today, many would feel as if the third monk wasted his life. What's he good for? What's he contributing to society? Or to the GDP? Or to the causes of justice? Why does he even matter?

Yet here he is, the exemplar in this weird, ancient story, calling to us from another place, culture, and time, asking us to reexamine our true purpose.

It's not that, in our day, we never see solitude or stillness as valuable. We likely think of them as necessary acts of "self-care." Yet we primarily view them as means to the end of more exertion, more rigor, more impact. They are merely fuel for a machine whose chief purpose is output and productivity. But this story implies that solitude and silence are our orienting goals, the re-humanizing rhythms that teach us that we are not, in fact, machines, but creatures—creatures with faults, limits, beauty, and worth, creatures made to dwell deeply with God.

If we see solitude and stillness primarily as a means to more productivity, we will try to get by with just enough to keep us going and no more. But if these practices are essential to our very being, to our purpose and humanity, then we will orient our work and our days, our weeks and our years, around them. These countercultural, seemingly wasteful things will become our first, most important, order of business. The third monk will turn out to be our surprise hero.

To be sure, most of us will not—and should not—follow him into a life of complete withdrawal. We have responsibilities: jobs to do, neighbors to care for, children to raise, meetings to attend, and dinner to make. Yet the Desert Fathers and Mothers remind us, in their lives and their sayings, that we are created, first and foremost, for connection with the Source of all life. When we lose this primary connection, even for the sake of important and needful things, we wither. We find ourselves, like the first and second monk, overcome by weariness, flailing in spirit, and unable to carry out our purpose.

To be restored will inevitably take some intentionality and require us to embrace different practices that shape how we use our time. This is difficult work. But the only way to grow deep in these weary lands is to be still and silent long enough to put our ear to the ground and hear the rumblings of our hearts, our longings, and our Creator. If we are to learn to see ourselves and the world clearly, we have to have moments, days, and seasons when we let the silt of our lives settle.

II.

The fact that so many of us feel weary or burned out—the fact that this phenomenon is common enough to be splashed across headlines and memes—points to the reality that much of our exhaustion isn't simply self-made. It's not merely that we aren't disciplined enough, or that we have not figured out how to life-hack our way into flourishing. It's that to live a life of depth at a humane pace is to struggle against our culture's current. And that is difficult to do.

The Catholic philosopher Josef Pieper says that our culture encourages what he calls a "world of 'total work,'" in which prizing leisure seems suspect, even immoral. The temptation is to be always on, always engaged, rushed, and productive. We think of leisure as a luxury for the lucky few or for a rare vacation—we see it as lounging poolside with piña coladas. In Greek, however, the word for leisure, *skole,* is the same word from which we get the word *school.* Leisure, in this sense, is not understood as indulgence or opulence. It is, instead, spaciousness in our schedule. It's preserving enough breadth in our day to think, to be curious, and to learn. It is saying no to many things so we can say yes to others—especially if that yes is not to another productive task but to sitting on our couch and reading, or hanging out with a close friend, or sitting in silence alone. This spacious time *schools* us. It allows us, as Heraclitus says, to listen "to the essence of things."[4]

Gregory the Great, the celebrated pope of the sixth century, was born wealthy but left his family business to become a monk and an ascetic. He hoped to live a quiet life entirely dedicated to prayer and contemplation. He wanted the life of the third monk. Instead, he was called from his monastic life into the difficult service of a needy and feuding church. When he took up his office as pope, the western half of the Roman Empire had effectively collapsed. The political order was fractured. Gregory's work was cut out for him. In spite of having much to do, he recognized that he could not continue to fulfill his purpose and his call to reform the church without regular reprieve.

His practice, and his counsel to others, was to embrace periods of retreat for the sake of contemplation, even amid a life full of activity and service. Gregory writes, "For holy men . . . are sent and go forth as lightnings, when they come forth from the retirement of contemplation, to the public life of employment. . . . [From] the secrecy of inward meditation, they spread forth into the wide space of active life." But they must always return to solitude and stillness. He likens it to a man going out to work in a cruel winter storm and then coming back home to warm up by the fire. "They would freeze too speedily," Gregory says, "amid their outward works, good though they be, did they not constantly return with anxious earnestness to the fire of contemplation."[5]

This rhythm of engagement and withdrawal described by the ancients is still available to us today in our era of traffic jams and TikTok, but it must be continually sought. Each day, we are sent from a place of security, warmth, and quiet rest in God into a world that is often convulsive, raging, and tumultuous. We immerse ourselves in this world, as observers, as learners, as workers, as citizens, as parents, as friends, as those who love and serve our neighbors, as those seeking truth, peace, and justice. But then we get the heck out of Dodge, through intentional times of stillness, rest, and prayer, to warm ourselves again in the "fire of contemplation."

For most of us, this will not look like long silent retreats. For all of us, it will certainly look different than it did for Gregory. But we start small and start somewhere. In my own life, spacious days are too few and far between. *Skole* seems fleeting. Yet, I try to take a few minutes each day, a day each week, and a longer period each year to intentionally seek time of rest, stillness, and solitude. This looks like turning off my phone and turning my attention to the depths of God. It looks like sitting on my back porch silently. It looks like taking a nap, writing in a journal, or booking a day at the Catholic retreat center near my house.

For all of us, in the ways we can stay in the cell of our actual lives, we can warm our souls in the fire of God's presence—a fire we do not start with our own eagerness and energy, but a fire that is waiting for us.

These intentional rhythms of engagement and withdrawal are, most notably, seen in the life of Jesus. Throughout the Gospels, a clear pattern emerges. Jesus immersed himself in the world. He was surrounded by crowds—people touching him, people needing things from him, people adoring him and criticizing him, people trying to entrap him, people who were demanding and needy, people who were scary and angry. He had all the reason in the world to be weary. Yet we see him, time and time again, engaging the crowd with compassion, showing up and working, healing, and preaching.

And we see him, time and time again, quite literally fleeing from the crowds to hide out alone. He pursued silence and solitude like a thirsty man pursues water. It was his constant orienting activity.

On one level, what a waste of time and talent! Every hour he spent alone on the side of a mountain was an hour of his short public ministry where he wasn't preaching or healing. Each moment he chose solitude a leper wasn't being healed, a hungry person was not being fed, an unjust empire was marching on. This man who could raise the dead and quell storms spent much of his time doing seemingly nothing useful at all. Still, he thought these hours and days of quiet withdrawal were worth putting off everything else he could have been doing.

This rhythm adopted by Jesus shows us the true purpose of contemplation. Jesus—like the Desert Fathers and Mothers—did not withdraw because he was a misanthrope who wanted to get away from the burden of people. The point of withdrawal is to watch and wait for communion with God.

We tend to think lofty phrases like "the contemplative life" describe something far removed from our quotidian world—being tucked away in a hermitage or monastery, constantly enraptured in prayer. But a contemplative life is simply one that seeks to remain open to the constant presence of God. Our task in growing deep is to learn the pedestrian graces that allow an ordinary life to also be a life of contemplation. What fuels resilience—what will keep us going when life gets hard and tiring—isn't willpower or guilt. It is neither self-empowerment nor self-flagellation. It is learning to practice silence and solitude. It is learning to take up gentle rhythms of engagement and withdrawal that restore and renew us at the Source.

III.

In my own time of aridity, I craved withdrawal. At least, I thought I did. I said I did. I fantasized about hushed, spacious days, deep silence, and empty hours. Yet when I did manage to get a spare hour in my actual day, I found myself unable to settle down, unable to quiet my insides. My brain thrashed about looking for something—anything!—to distract me. My mind would present a dozen tasks to do, or a question I just *had* to google immediately. I would recall a news story I'd wanted to read or a text I needed to return. My nervous system was amped up. My brain was twitchy and addled. I didn't know what to do with myself. And so, by habit, I turned to the digital circus always waiting for me with its bug zapper glow, right in my pocket.

When life feels on top of us, calls to stillness and withdrawal can feel a little like asking a drowning person to complete a homework assignment. The bad news is that these times when we feel most depleted are when it is easiest to collapse into noise and distraction, which makes us, in the end, more depleted. We are like a drunk man drinking ocean water to quench his thirst.

It's why the nights when I feel most exhausted and overwhelmed are exactly when I catch myself doomscrolling too late or scouring online comments, looking for a dopamine hit in all the wrong places. It's why our whole culture feels marked by this strange combination of being both bored and restless, weary yet wired.

Blaise Pascal famously said that "the sole cause of man's unhappiness is that he does not know how to stay quietly in his room."[6] (This quote is, ironically, passed around often on crowded and noisy social media platforms.) In his work, Pascal reflects on the idea of *ennui*—a French word that came to mean "boredom" in English, but that originally meant something more all-encompassing, something akin to "weariness," or my favorite definition: "fed-up-ness."[7]

We are full to the brim with fed-up-ness. I think "fed-up-ness" may even be a better cultural diagnosis than terms like burnout or languishing. We are fed up with noise and hurry, fed up with politics and rancor, fed up with feeling as though we are always running hard yet running behind, fed up with our neighbors and even ourselves.

For Pascal, a key symptom of ennui—fed-up-ness—is that we resist rest, even though we are deeply weary. We compulsively fill silence with noise, solitude with crowds, and stillness with hurry.[8] This forms both individuals and a society that are simultaneously exhausted and unable to rest. Instead of ever taking time to let the silt settle, we run to frivolous distractions that, over time, cultivate a profound inattention to the world. Pascal, writing in the seventeenth century, cites billiard tables as the distraction of choice. Today it would be glowing screens.

Ennui emerges, he writes, "from the depths of our hearts, where it is naturally rooted."[9] This is why I fill up each empty moment, even though I claim to crave stillness. The discipline needed for contemplation, Pascal suggests, is not only a discipline of scheduling—of having open time in the day or week. It is, more powerfully, a fight within ourselves, within our very souls. It is the struggle to enter the pain and vulnerability of boredom, uncertainty, and quiet. It is the discipline of learning to remain still and attentive, which requires training—and, in our moment, significant retraining.

Distraction and restlessness are obviously not inventions of the digital age. The fifth-century monk Germanus complained that it was difficult to focus and pray because "the mind is constantly tangled up in this ignorant and struggling state, always reeling around and stumbling into things like it's drunk."[10] Who can't relate to that?

Today, however, in a way Germanus could never have imagined, we can remain seemingly alone in our room, yet still have constant, glowing access to crowds, noise, and hurry.

What smartphones often take from us are those little moments of margin in our days, natural times of silence and stillness that we once took for granted: a few minutes' break between tasks, waiting in traffic or in the grocery line, going to the bathroom, walking from one place to another, lying down in bed at night. These tiny moments were hardly noticeable to us before they were snatched away, filled with information and entertainment.

Being constantly filled up makes us empty. We cannot, as a species, thrive without blank spaces in our day. I suspect it is no accident that reports of burnout and exhaustion have surged as smartphones have become ubiquitous. We can't get away from Pascal's billiard tables now.

Fifteen years ago, in his book *The Shallows: What the Internet Is Doing to Our Brains,* Nicholas Carr argued that the internet was rewiring our brains to take in many small snatches of information—to the point that we lose the ability to sit with one conversation or keep up with a long argument.[11] The titanic disaster that this represents for theological rigor, spiritual practices, and the contemplative life cannot be overstated. It may appear "a historical chasm separates the temptations of desert monks from those of young people surfing the internet," Daniel Silver writes in a piece for *The Point* magazine. But our "culture of entertainment may be the driest spiritual desert Satan has devised as of yet."[12]

Apprenticeship to Jesus, like apprenticeship to any craft, requires us to train not just our bodies or beliefs, but also our attention. Over time and with practice, we learn what to notice and what to ignore. We hone what occupies our imaginations and directs our gaze.

Unlike the Desert Fathers and Mothers, we are not surrounded by a savage, empty wasteland but by a profusion of devices the likes of which the world has never seen. This constant noise and connectivity of online life kills our capacity for wonder and astonishment, for listening to what stalks the silences. If we want to become people able to attend to those things that are deepest and most real, we have to intentionally rewire our brains, to sober up our drunken minds, and to break our addiction to distraction. We must learn to practice silence and stillness and to give sustained attention to our material and embodied lives.

IV.

"When the door of the steam baths is continually left open, the heat inside rapidly escapes through it," wrote fifth-century ascetic Diadochus of Photiki. "Likewise the soul, in its desire to say many things, dissipates its remembrance of God through the door of speech."[13] In the digital world, we now have an opportunity to keep the "door of speech" open at every moment of every day and night.

I am hesitant to tell my "going off social media" story. So many writers tell a version of this story that it now feels cliché, or worse, self-congratulatory. In my case, though, the decision to go offline was entirely other people's idea. I refer to it now—somewhat but not entirely joking—as "the intervention."

I have a group of friends who live all over the country. For several years, we made a habit of meeting once a month on Zoom and gathering in person a couple of times a year. In these in-person gatherings, we sat in a circle and talked about what's happening in our lives. The real stuff, the hard stuff.

One time we met in person when I was writing weekly for *The New York Times.* I told them how tired I was, how I didn't know how to keep juggling marriage, kids, and work. My youngest was only two at the time, still in diapers. I was overwhelmed. "I just don't know how to keep going," I said. They listened compassionately for a long time. Then it was their turn to speak.

Four of my friends joined together in a plan. My friend Andy spoke first. I needed to get off Twitter, he said, pointedly but kindly. His tone made it clear it wasn't exactly a suggestion. The current issue of my life, he explained, cannot boil down to time management. It was deeper. I needed what he called "energy management." It wasn't just that social media took up too much time. It was that it sucked up emotional, spiritual, and creative energy that I deeply needed in order to keep going and to thrive. The fastest, easiest way to regain that energy was to cut the cord.

But they knew that I had tried before to kick my Twitter habit and had always gotten sucked back in. I needed a way, they told me, to resist social media that was not reliant on my puny willpower.

When the friends who are supposed to be your sounding board in life all gang up together to tell you to stop something, there's not much to do but listen to them. So I asked my husband and another close friend and colleague for help. They changed my password on Twitter (now X)—I don't know what it is to this day. The same site we used to block pornography in our home we now also use to block social media on my computer. So when I try to peek at the chatter online—and I still sometimes do—a screen pops up with an inspirational message, like some perky digital rehab counselor I want to punch in the mouth.

In the intervention, my friends encouraged me, "Just try it for four months or so, then you can get back on if you want to." For the first few months, I still thought in 280-character bites. I still looked everywhere for distraction. And I missed social media all the time. As I drifted to sleep each night, my brain would reflexively compose pithy tweets and posts, ones I knew would kill online—but alas, there was nowhere to share them. By month four, I had not found deep internal stillness or uninterrupted bliss, but I began to clearly recognize that I was detoxing from something poisonous. There was a physical change in my body, as if I were withdrawing from a drug, or powering down somehow, becoming more human. I felt calmer. My shoulders relaxed. My thoughts quieted. So I decided to keep going.

I haven't been on Twitter now for four years, though I do text a colleague (the friend who knows my password) if I need to post something for my work. I still occasionally post on Facebook or Instagram. Admittedly, I am a bit of a cheater. The pull to rejoin the constant din of online life has weakened, though. I feel freer. And when there is a major event in my life or in the world, I do not rush to dash out my thoughts. Instead, I'm able to sit, to process, to grieve, to think. I'm able to be silent, to leave the steam bath door closed. And that feels like a gift that I nearly gave up.

I don't think everyone has to withdraw as much as I did. For me, though, going dark online was an essential part of my overall treatment for burnout and aridity. I had to figure out how to be an informed citizen while also intentionally, doggedly extricating myself from noise.

It isn't as simple as saying that iPhones and social media *cause* aridity. After all, this phenomenon was described by Christians millennia ago. It's more that, in the desert, when nourishment feels in short supply, one must learn to notice and lap up every bit of goodness, truth, and beauty around us. Instead of doing this, I had developed habits of distraction that starved me slowly. I trained myself over time to crave turbulence so much that I was unable to let the silt of my life and thoughts settle.

If I was going to heal and grow deep, I did not primarily need my *thinking* to change. I needed—and I continuously need—my habits of digital consumption to be retrained. I had to get back to some kind of contemplation, some "remembrance of God."

Christians cannot truly be an alternative people—a witness to a different way of being in the world—if we simply have different beliefs than our neighbors but all the same digital habits and practices. One of my favorite essays of the last decade is Andrew Sullivan's article in *New York* magazine, "I Used to Be a Human Being." He writes about his deep immersion in social media and his eventual escape from it into a life of more silence. "If the churches came to understand that the greatest threat to faith today is not hedonism but distraction," he concludes, "perhaps they might begin to appeal anew to a frazzled digital generation."[14]

When everyone in a room is shouting, the most radical thing a person can do is be silent. In the same way, often the most radical thing the church can do now is to be anonymously faithful and counterculturally quiet. It is *not* to seek to be influencers who are always heard and noticed. It is *not* to constantly assert ourselves or proclaim our opinions, however brave and prophetic that may feel at moments. Our task as a church is to help people learn to be human again, to learn to be a community capable of contemplation and capable of going deep.

The internet keeps us ever engaged and often enraged. It keeps us clamoring for provocation and unnuanced arguments. It keeps us from noticing the world around us and within us. I'm convinced that what the world most needs is not any more tweets, any more posts, any more noise, but instead a people capable of closing the steam bath door. The task of the church is to become a community that has been so formed by God that we can think deeply, read deeply, work deeply, listen deeply, create deeply, and love deeply.

Amma Syncletica spoke of the need to carry the desert with us wherever we may go.[15] This means that we learn to live our lives, even here in our noisy, frenetic world, differently. We take up small practices of silence and stillness, intentionally and consistently. We are re-created in the silences to be a different sort of person as we walk through our world.

7

Brace the Wall

persevering amid doubt and disorientation

I.

I am by nature a questioner and a doubter. As a priest and a writer, I have studied and wrestled with the scriptures. I believe that Jesus died and was resurrected from the dead. I have read and written defenses of the historic accuracy of the Christian faith.

Still, every few months, I'll lie in bed at night and think: *Is any of this real?* It's just how I'm wired. I tend to doubt everything, from whether I made the best choice of entree at a restaurant to whether airplanes are actually safe.

Yet for all of us, in times of aridity, doubt often grows louder. Even those things that once felt solid and reliable can suddenly wobble and shift. If we are to sustain faith over a lifetime, we inevitably must learn how to face doubt.

Some doubt arises from an honest accounting that there's so much we just can't know. We are each small, fallible, and limited in our perspective. Any encounter with true beauty or transcendence always contains mystery—things higher than we can fully understand.

As Christians, we seek something—or rather someone—knowing, from the jump, that our reach will exceed our grasp. No matter how supposedly right our theology, how good our deeds or doctrine, we must leave room for what the artist and theologian Jeremy Begbie calls God's "uncontainability."[1] This is God, after all. Not a formula, a religious relic, or sociological phenomenon, but the maker of ocean tides and black holes, the inventor of platypuses and boll weevils, the one whose very breath birthed the laughter of children.

Christians, of course, believe that this deep mystery can, and has, revealed himself to us. We know God because God drew near and lived among human beings. The uncontainable infinite "dwindled to infancy," as Gerard Manley Hopkins wrote.[2] We have words to say about God because the Word became flesh.

Even so, we can't fully know, or believe in, the truth beneath all things. Not only are we limited, we are sinful. We don't like the idea of having a boss, much less a judge of all heaven and earth. And of course, God simply does not explain himself entirely. He did not drop a systematic theology book from the heavens to answer all our questions. He has no 24-hour customer service hotline. Instead, he invites us to enter into and endure a mystery.

I find some of the ways that Christians discuss doubt lacking. On the one hand, doubt can be painted as a disaster, as sinful and wrong. On the other, it can be portrayed as fashionable, subversive, brave, or original. In reality, doubt is simply a fact of human existence, like sadness or fear. Doubt can become disordered, unhelpful, misleading, or overwhelming, like any other human thought or feeling. For the most part, though, it is a normal response to living a full life and can even be a useful motivation for seeking truth.

Because mystery is real, and because we live in an enchanted and enchanting universe, faith and doubt remain ever entwined in the human experience. And lest one assume that my comfort with doubt is some newfangled innovation—a softening of convictions for our skeptical age, or the product of the flaccid faith of an overly permissive female priest—we see similar ideas throughout the Christian tradition. Even a strict and somber seventeenth-century Puritan, Obadiah Sedgwick, writes that faith and doubt are "not opposed as life and death, where the presence of the one determinately concludes the total absence of the other." They exist more like currents of heat and cold in the same room—"both may and do meet in the same person" at the same time, he concludes.[3]

There will always be times, in every life, when seeking to know God feels like walking in a fog toward God-knows-what. There will be times when God seems like someone we can't live with and can't live without. To walk as an apprentice of Jesus is to live in a state of faith that constantly confesses, in words from the Gospel of Mark, "I believe; help my unbelief!"[4] There are seasons—sometimes long seasons—in every Christian life where niggling questions roar to the surface. We wonder, *Is what I believe actually true? Can our claims about God support the weight of my life?* These questions are not something to fear or to avoid. They can even become a way to new depths of faith. If God is real, he is strong enough to bear the force of honest questions.

My longtime friend Nate, a writer and an accomplished editor, once told me something that changed how I see my work. "Writers," he said, "don't just find their voice. They find it and lose it, and find it again, maybe slightly different, and lose it again, and find it and lose it and find it." On and on. This is what happens over the long stretch if you persist in any craft. And it's true of the Christian life as well. We don't simply find faith, once and for all. We find it and lose it and find it again. We believe and doubt and believe. We sort through what is essential and what is not. We sift through the ways our culture or upbringing has warped our understanding of the gospel. We learn. We repent. We rethink.

To be clear, I do not mean that we are constantly in and out of the church, or that we change our views on God as casually as we change our clothes. What I mean is that conversion—the transformation of our hearts and minds—is not just a moment but the project of a lifetime. We are converted and converted and converted, day by day, sometimes hour by hour.

II.

John of the Cross wrote that the dark night of the soul produces a particular strain of doubt, which he called the "spirit of blasphemy."[5] This is not so much doubting that God exists, but instead doubting that he can be trusted. We look at this aching world with children in hospice, with families swept away in a flood, with the pain of our own life, and in some wordless place within us, we wonder if God is, in fact, a monster or a tyrant.

In times when God seems distant or silent, this type of doubt can become sharp and overpowering. The spirit of blasphemy constantly shows us everything wrong in the world and in our own life. It insists that if there is a God, he must be cruel and out to get us or impotent and apathetic.

Amid my own struggles with this kind of doubt, my medicine was a stout and steady dose of the Psalms. They egged me on and kept me going. They showed me how to pray. Reciting the Psalms, both with my church and alone in my room, reminded me that yelling at God about our anger, our doubt, and our complaints is perhaps one of the most faithful moves we can make.

When I turned forty-four years old, I decided to spend the whole year reading, re-reading, and meditating on Psalm 44, a lament that blames God for Israel's humiliation and suffering. It begins by reflecting with joy, worship, and just a splash of nostalgia on how good and kind God is to his people—or rather, how good and kind he used to be. "But now," the Psalmist turns, "you have rejected and humbled us." He goes on like this, making God seem worse and worse. "You sold your people for a pittance, gaining nothing from their sale." He adds, like a prosecutor laying out his case, that the fault lies with God, not people: "All this came upon us, though we had not forgotten you; we had not been false to your covenant. Our hearts had not turned back; our feet had not strayed from your path. But you crushed us and made us a haunt for jackals; you covered us over with deep darkness."[6] These were the words I meditated on, week in and week out, for months.

One helpful thing I discovered through this practice is that no normal person should read a Psalm this depressing as frequently as I did that year. (At least throw in some Psalm 23 "goodness and mercy will follow me" as a chaser.) If someone wrote Psalm 44 as a worship song today, it wouldn't sell. If we said these things about God in church, well-meaning people would worry for our souls. Yet here it is, unapologetically included in the church's oldest prayer book. Reading this Psalm, day after day, I figured that I couldn't say much worse to or about God than the Psalmist already had, so I may as well voice my darkest doubts.

Psalm 44 ends in an unexpected way, however. Nearly the whole Psalm reads like a rant against God that the late antitheist Christopher Hitchens might have applauded. But then, in the end—twist!—the Psalmist calls on God to save him: "Rise up and help us; rescue us because of your unfailing love."[7]

Your unfailing love?!? The author just spent eighteen verses chewing God out, only to end by talking about a love that, apparently, he believes never actually fails.

The Old Testament scholar Walter Brueggemann notes that Psalms of lament follow a pattern of orientation, disorientation, and new orientation or reorientation—and that this reflects the pattern of the Christian life.[8] We begin in a state of orientation, in which we know, or at least think we know, how things work. Our lives make sense. God seems near. This is the illumination, the sweetness. And then, disorientation. We don't know where we are, where God is, or how to go on. Eventually, after this long middle, comes reorientation: a new, more complex, and deeper way of knowing God. This is what's happening in Psalm 44. The Psalmist laments his lost faith in one breath and exercises faith in the next. He holds anger and trust together with no seeming contradiction. He seems at the point of despair, but his final word in this Psalm speaks of God's kindness.

This Psalm was my prayer that whole, long forty-fourth year, and it became my blueprint for holding both honesty and trust, aridity and ardor, doubt and faith. The Psalmist does not deny his pain. He does not resort to pat answers. He's looking for action on the part of God. He yells, "Wake up! Come and help us!" He asks for, even demands, a love that will set things to rights.

Apparently, God does not hold this against him.

Psalm 44 comes up again, in the New Testament. Paul quotes it verbatim in his letter to the Romans, in a meditation on God's unfailing love. But that final note of trust from the Psalm—the love part—is not the part that Paul quotes in Romans.

In chapter 8, Paul erupts in ebullience about how kind, how near, how good God is: "Who shall separate us from the love of Christ? Shall trouble or hardship or persecution or famine or nakedness or danger or sword?" Then, right in the middle of his worship chorus, he quotes this angry lament from Psalm 44: "For your sake we face death all day long; we are considered as sheep to be slaughtered."[9] It comes off like a record scratch.

Paul is writing to the Christians in Rome, to people facing intense persecution and slaughter because of their faith. He sees in their story the same suffering and pain the Psalmist was grieving and grappling with. So Paul quotes this Psalm, which his readers would have known by heart. They, too, felt like sheep led to slaughter.

Paul, however, doesn't end his thought (as the Psalmist does) by asking God to wake up and rescue them. He assumes God is awake and alive and has already rescued them decisively in the person of Jesus: "For I am convinced that neither death nor life, neither angels nor demons, neither the present nor the future, nor any powers, neither height nor depth, nor anything else in all creation, will be able to separate us from the love of God that is in Christ Jesus our Lord."[10] For Paul, the evidence for (or against) God's unfailing love is not whether he and his fellow believers are rescued from death or not. Instead, he looks to the life, death, and resurrection of Jesus. That is his proof that God is not in fact a monster who sells out his people.

But this "love of God that is in Christ Jesus our Lord" is a strange love, a suffering love. At times, it's a confusing love. In that way, it rewrites any simplistic idea of love that we may have picked up from pop culture or even church culture.

One of the gifts of aridity is that, in desolation, our naïve, unexamined ideas about God, and about what God's love ought to look like, are dashed against the rocks of reality so that a truer, more enduring trust might be built from the wreckage. Psalm 44 is a brutal short story of that experience. With the Psalmist, we must learn, again and again, to rage and weep at the silent sky yet return to a God whose love does not fail. With the Psalmist, we lose our faith and find it anew, sometimes in the span of the very same prayer.

III.

Many Christians have written on doubt, but the author Andy Crouch offered one of the most helpful reflections on the idea that I've heard. "I cannot imagine living an aware, awake, curious life in the world without doubt," Crouch said. "It just seems to me to be part of a kind of exploration of the world." He mentions that characters in the Bible universally seem to wrestle with deep doubt. But, he adds, it is key to understand that "you cannot actually practice your doubts, you can only practice a faith."[11]

He explains further, "You are going to live by some set of beliefs about what's really true about the world." Of course, this belief may be that God isn't real, or that God isn't trustworthy, or that we are on our own in a vast, indifferent universe. But this is a *claim* about the world, not a doubt.

All of us live each day practicing a faith. It is unavoidable. We practice our faith in how we think, in how we spend our time and money, in how we use our bodies, in where we look for moral guidance or authority or hope, in what we say yes and no to, in how we pray or don't pray, in how we spend our days.

I have a friend who says her official faith is "I don't know, and neither do you." That's all fine and good, but she, like all of us, ends up living as if *something* is knowable and true. She still has to decide whether to show up to a church on a Sunday morning or sleep in. She still has to decide whether or not to tell a white lie. She still has to decide what to teach her children about the meaning of life and what kind of moral duty they have to others (and why). She has to decide what the good is and if it can ever be arduous. She inevitably practices a faith—some bedrock belief in unprovable claims—in a thousand small and large decisions. We all do. We all bet our lives on something.

So where does this leave us? If doubt is a normal, inevitable part of faith, yet we cannot practice doubt, the question for Christians then becomes: How do we continue to practice faith with honesty and integrity amid doubt?

The ancient monks in the desert faced their own doubts and questions. They sometimes doubted if they had made the right choice to embrace their vocation and strange way of life. Their sayings mention other (usually unspecified) doubts, things they did not understand, things they struggled to believe. They often referred to these as "perplexities."[12]

They saw doubt and questions as a typical part of the life of faith. But they also warned against facing them alone. They advised those in doubt to seek out trusted guides for help and counsel. These guides were those who'd proven their trustworthiness and wisdom over time and had kept faith amid suffering and struggle.

A lesser-known Desert Father, Abba Job, said that a person who experiences "doubt about scripture and does not come to the wise ones and learn" is like a wall that breaks under the shock of a flood.[13] When doubt inevitably comes, he suggests, the wall of our faith needs bracing. We need supports, reinforcements, sandbags; we need others to hold us up.

One misunderstanding that we in modernity have is the assumption that in order for faith to be authentic, it must be constructed and sustained individually. It must be fueled by our own self-discovery. Our own voice and intuitions, above all others, must guide us.

But the world has no freethinkers. None of us, from the most faithful believer to the most ardent skeptic, believe or disbelieve on our own. We are influenced by what those around us find credible or incredible, believable or unbelievable. We are shaped, often without recognizing it, by ideas passed to us from others and from those who came before us.

The Christian faith cannot be sustained over a lifetime simply by our own strength or our best thinking. In his explanation of baptism, Anglican theologian N. T. Wright said, "Belief is actually not an isolated individual thing. I don't believe in a little box all by myself. Yes, I have my own particular take on things, but the great creeds say, '*We* believe.' Belief is something that actually we do together."[14]

For the desert monks, the "wise ones" who help brace vulnerable faith against the flood were people they knew and who knew them. These were elders and leaders—spiritual guides—in their community whom they could sit down with, face to face, and to whom they could unburden the struggles of their soul.[15] These trusted mentors helped sift, clarify, and address one's perplexities.

We need this as well when we face perplexities and doubts today. The popular term "deconstruction" is a single word that covers such a maddeningly wide range of experiences that I'm skeptical of its value—it could mean questioning, deepening, reevaluating, or discarding faith or the church. There are so many vast and varied motivations that might drive a reexamination of our faith. We need wise people who love us to help locate the source of our struggle, to trace the various threads of our perplexities.

Are our doubts rooted in honest intellectual questions that require study and a rigorous, learned response? Or are they born of church hurt or religious trauma that we need to voice, grieve, work through (with God and others), and heal from? Do they stem from temptation or a repulsion at the ethical demands that faith may lay on us? Do they come from a false understanding of the faith presented by a particular modern subculture—for instance, a syncretism of faith and American politics? Or do they arise from disappointment or anger with God?

Doubts or perplexities are not just one thing that requires one stock response—we need help to unsnarl the tangle of questions, fears, confusion, and sorrows in our minds and hearts. Just as physical health cannot be sustained over a lifetime without seeing good doctors, our faith cannot endure for long without those trusted "wise ones" who faithfully practice the cure of souls.

We need others to hear, shape, and help address our questions. We need others to identify what threatens to buckle the wall of our faith—the various stresses on it and fissures in it. We need others to fortify us and help make us resilient.

IV.

There was a time when, in my imagination, the story of Christianity went something like this: Jesus died on the cross for my sins. And now, jumping over two thousand years, I believe in him and "ask him into my heart." It was almost an entirely individual story. There was no need for anything other than simply me and Jesus. No need for a church.

But this story makes smaller what Christ has done. Those who brace the wall of our faith are not only those we personally know. We learn the craft of faith from countless other Christians who have walked this way ahead of us.

This does not mean they are above critique or criticism. It does not mean we cannot question what we've received. It does mean, however, that we cannot self-generate a sustaining faith. And it means that those who went before us ought to be allowed to question and critique us—that our assumptions and moment in history are as open to criticism as theirs.

Medieval Christian thinkers made a distinction between *fides qua creditur* (the faith with which we believe) and *fides quae creditur* (the faith that we believe).[16] The faith with which we believe is personal and subjective—we do the believing ourselves. No one can do it for us, obviously. But the faith that is believed is corporate and independent of us. It is the faith into which we are received, the faith of the communion of saints over time, the faith that supports and sustains us and has been passed down to us. It is a big room that I did not build, that other people got to before me, and it sits outside of me, steady and sturdy, even as my own individual faith—the faith by which I believe—is intermittent, wobbly, waxing and waning.

I am not saying that anyone should begrudgingly mutter the creed in church with fingers crossed or muddle through a religious faith *simply* because their parents did. If I ever come to truly disbelieve the story of Jesus, there is integrity in leaving the faith and finding a new one to practice. Still, how I feel about my faith, how ardent or dubious or confused I may be from day to day or week to week, varies wildly.

In seasons of aridity, I'm comforted that there are weeks when I can simply show up at church, weak and wounded, and rely on the faith of those around me. We stand and say, "We believe in God the Father . . ." However I feel, this is what we believe. Together. I walk into a room where others dwell.

In my children's school, art instruction explicitly involves learning to imitate others. Their art teachers don't simply lay out the materials and let the students go at it. The children first do renderings of other great works. Inch by inch, they study and painstakingly duplicate the works of O'Keeffe, Rembrandt, or Cassatt. It isn't that they never let the kids make their own unique work (they have other times when they create originals), but they assume that what will best teach these kids to paint is to have a long, detailed lesson from the great artists of history—to literally copy them. Once they've sat with the work of a better, older artist for a long while, they might begin to understand their own craft and work.

This is how I feel about the historic liturgy. I say the prayers of others, prayers that have been wrought in faith and doubt, pain and tears, over time, and this teaches me how to pray. It is not on my own exhausted shoulders to constantly innovate my practice of prayer. I can render others' words as my own. I can copy them, and in this way, I can pray with them across time, and they can teach me to pray. This braces the wall of my faith; it holds me up when the flood of my own grief, disbelief, or weariness flows fiercely.

V.

Looking at the global and historic church, we discover that there is no question that hasn't been asked, no doubt that has not cropped up, no spiritual pain or disappointment that has not been borne by others.

A corrupt, cruel, spineless, and politically captive church? Christians have dealt with this before and worked (sometimes even died) for reform. Intellectual and philosophical questions assailing our beliefs? This is nothing new. The problem of pain—of following a God who allows immense suffering in our lives and in the broader world? This has been faced, discussed, and written about by Christians for millennia. A morality out of step with our broader cultural assumptions and expectations? Others have known this well. A profound and enduring sense of God's absence? Saints throughout time have experienced this and lived to tell the tale.

The church has clearly and horrifically failed in innumerable ways across its history. Yet, in every age, in all sorts of cultures, there were faithful Christians who faced unspeakable evils, unanswerable questions, and unimaginable hardship and kept going, faithfully—even joyfully—persisting in the craft of faith. Their resilience isn't just inspiring. Their lives, writings, and prayers instruct me in how to become more resilient. I get to cheat off their tests when I'm facing my own. Their voices tell me to hold on, to keep going.

A deeper and broader understanding of the Christian faith does not make all our doubts or questions go away, but it pushes against the myopia of our contemporary moment and its intractable culture wars and debates. It lends confidence that the questions of our age are not as unique, original, or insurmountable as we may think. And it can fire our imagination to see how others have responded to similar challenges with honesty and steadfastness.

In my time of aridity, the fact that others, from so many times, cultures, and places, with so many temperaments, personalities, and passions, have struggled with doubt and despondency offered me a lifeline—or rather a lifeboat packed with others.

Let's take just one. Thérèse of Lisieux wrote in the nineteenth century that God allowed her "to be overwhelmed with darkness." She faced a profound struggle with disbelief. In her autobiography, she wrote: "He permitted my soul to be invaded by the thickest darkness, and . . . the thought of heaven, up until then so sweet to me, be no longer anything but the cause of struggle and torment. This trial was to last not a few days or a few weeks, it was not to be extinguished until the hour set by God Himself and this hour has not yet come."[17] She confessed to an older nun, "If you only knew what darkness I am plunged into. I don't believe in eternal life; I think that after this life there is nothing. Everything has disappeared on me, and I am left with love alone."[18] Yet, she said, she continued in the motions of faith. She wrote that Jesus "knows very well that while I do not have the joy of faith, I am trying to carry out its works at least."[19]

Not long after this, Thérèse died of tuberculosis. In one of her final prayers, she said, "I ask Jesus to draw me into the flames of His love, to unite me so closely with Him that He live and act in me."[20] Her sisters wrote that in her final moments she sighed, "Oh, I love Him! My God, I love You!" Then she raised her eyes, and her face became "an expression of total peace and sheer joy."[21]

Reflecting on Thérèse's life and struggles, the Catholic priest and theologian Tomáš Halík wrote, "Christian faith—unlike 'natural religiosity' and happy-go-lucky religiosity—is *resurrected faith.*" It is a "faith that has to die on the cross, be buried, and rise again—in a new form. This faith is a process—and it is possible for people to find themselves at different phases of this process at different moments of their lives."[22] Maybe faith must die and, by God's grace, be constantly made new and born again in us. Maybe this is part of learning to believe, again and again.

VI.

In one of my favorite podcasts on writing, *The Habit,* host Jonathan Rogers ends each interview asking his guests the same question: "Who are the writers that make you want to write?"

It's such a good question, because it's a way for writers—a vocation we often misunderstand as solitary—to locate themselves in the broader story of a craft. A writer's answer to the question may be writers she knows personally, or writers who were dead long before she was born. It may be someone similar to her or remarkably different.

A question I keep returning to, a question I hold on to to keep going in the Christian life, is: Who are the believers that make you want to believe?

Whose faithfulness makes you want to be faithful? Surround yourself with these people. Immerse yourself in a church, in a Christian community, whose (albeit imperfect) lives help you learn, see, and seek what is most true, good, and beautiful. Immerse yourself in thinkers throughout time who have asked the questions your soul is shouting and offered you new ones as well. Immerse yourself in the prayers of those who teach you to pray and the songs of those who dare you to sing. Immerse yourself in the stories of saints and works of art that help you to glimpse the wild dance of God in the world.

After I spend time with certain friends and mentors, I'll catch myself longing to know God like they do. Because the God they follow is kind and gentle, but never a pushover. They live as people who have known agony and ecstasy. They have been disappointed and have failed and failed and failed, yet still know themselves as beloved. To me, they are a walking, breathing apologetic. They make me want to believe.

Tellingly, Rogers's question is not about who makes it *easier* to write. Those who make a writer want to write may, in ways, make the craft more (not less) challenging—because they witness to a beauty that one has not yet mastered. They raise our standards.

In the same way, those who make me want to believe may not make it any less arduous to do so. They do not offer me a faith that costs little or assure me that God affirms whatever it is I already think. But they urge me to persist and to go deep, to seek a life of truth and beauty, to not give up.

They are around me each Sunday in the pews. I show up, maybe feeling angry, impatient, sorry for myself, distracted, or faithless. Yet they are there, still singing and speaking truth over me, praying for me, asking how I'm doing. We stand together and say the creed, and their voices carry my own. After the scripture is read, they say, "Thanks be to God," and their gratitude stands in for my reluctance. They offer me bread and wine and tell me that this is the presence of God, even if it seems God is nowhere to be found. Their faithfulness makes me want to be faithful. And maybe next week, I'll do the same for them.

8

All Smoke, All Flame

the culmination of Christian resilience

I.

The world-renowned cellist Pablo Casals was asked why he continued to practice his instrument four or five hours a day at eighty-three years old. "Because I think I am making progress," he replied.[1]

To devote oneself fully to any craft requires the effort of a lifetime. As long as there is breath in you, my husband reminds me when I'm most discouraged, God is not finished with you—his work continues in and through you. Our very pulse is a continued invitation to practice and deepen.

This is why perseverance and resilience are so valuable. They are the necessary conditions of enduring over a lifespan, which is the only real chance we have at growth in anything. The reason marriage is "till death do us part" is not because the initial flame of passion is so strong but because love requires so much time—a lifetime—to even sort of learn what it is to practice it. The reason any creative endeavor invites us to keep practicing as long as we can is because we may, as Casals said, still make new progress at each stage. The reason faith requires a lifetime is because the mysteries, depths, and grace of God are so inexhaustible that the pursuit of God each moment of our lives only begins to scratch their surface.

Perhaps our stories can only rightly be understood in retrospect, after years of uncertainty, after the long middle. We will not understand mile one till we get to mile one thousand. And every twist and turn is part of the way we must walk to get there.

II.

In an interview with Ezra Klein, Oliver Burkeman looks at how the modern quest for productivity hacks and meticulous control over our time leads to burnout and anxiety. No matter how clever the scheduling app, how helpful the time management philosophy, how organized our days and weeks may be, we are simply not in control of our lives. "I think that burnout is best understood as having the component of a lack of meaning," Burkeman said, "that you're not only working incredibly hard, but it doesn't seem to get you any closer to the imagined moment when you're actually going to feel on top of everything and in control—like you can relax at last."[2] Because we know that the end for us mortals is not that we gain total control over our lives. The end is death, the ultimate marker of our lack of control.

Most mornings, I turn over a fifteen-minute hourglass and sit in silence as it drains. When I watch the last bits of sand funnel quickly to the bottom, I sometimes feel a slight sense of panic. *That's me,* I think. *That's my life. It will run out.* And I want to stop time. I always feel I need more time.

As we age, we begin to understand more deeply that in our world—our families, our churches, our relationships, our careers—there are things that we may not see mended, problems that may not yet be solvable, injustices that may not be righted, griefs that may not be healed. At least not in our lifetime.

We face not only grief but a profound sense of futility. We ask: Is this it? What's it all for?

We experience futility, in part, because this feeling hits on something true about being human. Left to us, to our efforts and understanding, life really is futile. And we know it. Nothing lasts. The graveyard is full of indispensable people.

Christian faith does not shy away from this harsh reality. Monks of old encourage us to keep "the expectation of death daily before our eyes."[3] This practice is not meant to be dour or morbid, but to cultivate wisdom—to teach us that we cannot address our sense of futility by denying it, ignoring it, or fleeing from it. To attempt to do so is to live an anesthetized life.

In the book of Ecclesiastes (the perfect companion for those who are languishing), the teacher declares that everything—work, effort, pleasure, study, even religious faith—is *hevel.* This word, often translated "vanity," literally means vapor or smoke. In death, everything goes up in smoke.

All of our efforts, our hopes, our best attempts, in the end, dwindle to ash.

When it comes to my own work, I mean this quite literally. I generally do not think people should ever burn books. That said, I've burned every book I've ever written. It's a weird ritual that began unexpectedly with my first book.

Toward the end of the editing process, I had printed out a full manuscript to edit by hand. But then, once the book was finished, I still had the thick stack of paper on my desk. And what was I to do with it? Throw it away? I couldn't. Those pages represented too many hours of my life, too much heartache and fear and hope, to consign them to the recycle bin.

As an Anglican priest, liturgical practices have shaped my imagination indelibly (for better or worse). In liturgical churches, objects used in worship, like chalices or altar cloths, are never thrown away. When they are worn out or no longer needed, they are burned or buried. It is a way to honor the sacredness of materiality, the holiness of touchable things. Writing books is, for me, a practice of devotion. My work, however good or bad it may be, is in this sense a sacred object—part of my measly attempt at something like worship.

So at the end of any long writing project, my husband and I light a fire in our backyard fire pit, pour some champagne, and slowly, over hours, bit by bit, burn the last printed manuscript I edited. We pray for the readers of the book (you). We pray for its reception. We thank God it's over. And we laugh and talk about the week and sit silently watching bright flames quiet to embers.

It has become a happy tradition over the years. And a dual symbol for me. On one hand, all those printed words ascending in smoke feel like a prayer in themselves. All these ideas and sentences, both lovely and faulted, this editing and effort, self-disclosure and self-doubt, worries and words, rising to God like the incense we burn in church each Sunday, curling and twisting toward heaven. There's something glorious about it.

And at the same time, something sad. Something that admits futility, that speaks of our long defeat. These flames remind me that all of my effort, struggle, failures, and successes end in death. All these hours of work, all these early mornings and headaches and drafts and tears and cursing at the rafters and small moments of triumph, turn to ash. They go up in smoke and are gone. I cannot make them last. Years of my life, thousands of words, *hevel, hevel.* It is all *hevel.* It blows away with the shifting wind.

In the face of futility, the writer in Ecclesiastes grows profoundly disillusioned with life. "If all is 'vapor,' where can we find a fulcrum to gain leverage on the world?" writes theologian Peter Leithart. "The world keeps plodding along as it always has despite all our frantic efforts. The sun rises and sets, smiling pityingly at our self-important activities. The rivers flow into the sea, and the sea remains at the same level, whether we succeed spectacularly or lamentably fail."[4]

After pages and pages in which the teacher in Ecclesiastes laments the futility of all things, another voice, the author or narrator, speaks. He steps onto the stage with the final word. "Here is the conclusion of the matter," he says. "Fear God and keep his commandments, for this is the duty of all mankind."[5] And then, his imagination stretches beyond this life altogether to the horizon of eternity, promising that God will measure up and judge every last thing.

Life in the here and now is futile, he tells us, but life here and now is not the end of the story. The ultimate hope for the Christian isn't that we can maximize this one life we live. It is found in the hope that God takes the ashes of our futile efforts and, from those ashes, makes something eternal.

Embracing arduousness or staying in one's cell makes no sense unless we hold hope that our day, today, participates in an eternal story, an eternal good that we are part of. If this life is all we have, then when things get hard or boring or costly, the best thing is to quickly move on. But the Christian hope is that God will come, not to whisk us off to a faraway heaven, but to establish his kingdom here on earth—and our little work, our little practices, our arduous goods here somehow mysteriously take part in eternal goodness. The ashes give way to beauty.

III.

After speaking at a university in Southern California, I decided on a whim to cancel my flight and take a train back home, from L.A. to Austin. I love trains and the American Southwest. For years, I'd dreamed of combining the two. This was my chance.

I boarded Amtrak late at night and woke just as the sun was peeking over the desert horizon in Arizona. I spent all day staring out the window. And one thing kept surprising me. When I had imagined this trip beforehand, I'd thought that in the arid Southwest, there would be almost no life. I imagined my train slowly rumbling through a wasteland of sand and not much else. Instead, what I saw was so much strange abundance, so much surprising growth.

I wrote in my journal, listing what I saw: yucca, prickly pear, a meandering cow, shockingly tall saguaros, what I thought might be acacia trees, unidentified "pointy, spikey shrubs." "I expected desolation," I wrote. "But what an odd extra-terrestrial lusciousness right here. . . . Life quietly shocks, surprises, endures. Things grow—not occasionally, but everywhere. Autumn rains yield life, relentless, hardier than I ever expected."

There are things that grow in dry and weary lands. There are things that only grow there.

The various ways plants survive amid aridity intrigue me. Cacti can live because they've adapted to catch any available moisture out of the air. They take and use every hint of nourishment that comes their way. They waste nothing good. Acacia trees have taproots that plunge down as deep as one hundred feet to find water underground. The drier it is, the deeper their roots grow. Then there are resurrection plants, which seem to entirely wither and die, only to spring back to life as soon as they meet with any moisture. Botanists have seen some resurrection plants revive after they appeared to be dead for over a century. All it took was a trickle.

To survive in these arid lands, plants have to become doggedly and creatively resilient. And that is what I hope grows in me in seasons that seem spiritually and emotionally dry. "Delicate beauties are brief," writes Debra Rienstra, reflecting on plants that survive harsh landscapes. "What lasts is tough and unglamorous—tenacious, companioned to the wind."[6]

I want to grow in this kind of tenacity. I want to learn to drink deep any nourishment to be found. I want my roots to deepen and deepen until they find their source. I want to learn to be companioned to the wind.

When I lived in Pittsburgh for several years, in the grayest parts of late winter, I'd frequently go to Phipps Botanical Gardens, an oasis of life and lusciousness. They had a room there with an African tree grape from Namibia. In winter, it would lose its leaves, harden, and cease its aboveground growth. A sign placed beside it read: "I'm not dead, I'm dormant."

In the midst of my desert season, I complained to my spiritual director a lot. "I feel lost," I'd say. "I feel nothing is happening spiritually or creatively. I feel uncertain." She'd say something like, "Well, maybe just be lost for a while. Be uncertain. Be unsure anything is happening." In other words, be dormant. In dormancy, it looks like a plant is dying. But this is how it persists, and how it is reborn.

In the scriptures, time and time again, people meet with this reality. We see Moses living for decades in the dry, barren country of Midian. We find the Israelites wandering in the wastelands, living on manna and quail. And we discover Jesus in the harsh Judean desert, hungry and alone, with wild animals, encountering the devil.

It's easy now, with these stories frozen neatly in ink on the page, to see these trials as necessary, inevitable, even uplifting. They have a beginning, middle, and end. They've been pinned down on many a flannelgraph, rendered palatable by time and distance. But for those in the story, the time in arid places was a time of struggle, vulnerability, and temptation.

Yet in each case, something was happening deep below the surface of time. Something new was taking root and coming into being, growing out there where nothing else grew.

After decades of quiet, Moses was sent first to a burning bush and then into his work as a liberator and leader. The people of God were sent from the desert to the Promised Land to form a new nation and culture. Jesus overcame temptation in the desert and was propelled into his public ministry. In each case, the desert was a time of emptiness but also of renewal and formation for what came next. The desert may have felt like a place of desolation. And it was. But it was also the site of the slow work of God coming to pass.

Paul tells us in Romans that the whole of creation is groaning, aching for redemption, waiting for birth. Whatever it may feel like at any given moment, a sign hangs over each of us—our days and weeks—and over this whole weary world, telling us that though things may be dormant, they are not dead. God is yet at work, growing something in his church, his people, in all of creation, something beautiful, solid, and lasting. He is growing something, even in me. The desert, at last, will bloom.

IV.

Perhaps the most widely known story of the Desert Fathers and Mothers involves a strange, mystical vision of fire:

> Abba Lot went to see Abba Joseph and said to him, "Abba, as far as I can I say my little office, I fast a little, I pray and meditate, I live in peace and as far as I can, I purify my thoughts. What else can I do?" Then the old man stood up and stretched his hands towards heaven. His fingers became like ten lamps of fire and he said to him, "If you will, you can become all flame."[7]

At first glance, it may seem as if this story goes against all I have written. This book is about staying at the little, daily habits of faith, "as far as we can," as Abba Lot says. It's about how we grow in perseverance, steadfastness, and resilience, even when the fire of faith falters. Then, this story seems to say that if we truly desire it, we can be so unified with the presence of God that our very bodies will be utterly changed into fire.

It almost reads like a condemnation. Why does Joseph get to become all flame while we who are barely hanging on to our little prayers and little efforts get nothing but desert, a long day, and the hot sun? It's as if we are sitting, striking match after match, and Abba Joseph is showing off. He's looking at us like, "Why don't you just turn into fire already, you slacker?"

But as I sat with the Desert Fathers and Mothers over time, the meaning of this story began to shift for me. This story of Lot and

Joseph reminds me that resilience is not an end unto itself. The point of all of our lives is encounter and unity with the living God.

We are not merely left with our little habits and practices to muddle through this weary world until at last we die. There is meaning. There is transcendence. There is a God who is wildly at work in the world and in us. His desire for us is nothing less than to be united with himself. This is the God that scripture calls a consuming fire, the God that when his disciples were gathered on Pentecost suddenly showed up in falling flames and the deafening sound of wind. This is the God that rose from the dead.

Reflecting on this story of Lot and Joseph, the Orthodox priest John Garvey points out that Joseph is called "the old man" in the story. He says this reflects the idea of "an elder"—*geron* in Greek—a word "still used of wise monks and spiritual directors."[8] Garvey says this is to show that getting to this mystical fire takes patience and perseverance. It takes training over a lifetime, and maybe even beyond that. It takes walking through times when God feels distant and hard to get. It takes resilience.

Before this miraculous moment with Lot, Joseph had spent his whole life seeking God above comfort or the good life, or even a fiery spiritual experience. He did not stroll into the desert one day as a zealous young man and begin living his life in daily fireworks. He persevered, over time, in a tiny cell in a vast desert, daily dying to himself and, like Abba Lot, praying, fasting, seeking peace, purifying himself, as far as he could. Little by little, becoming who he was made to be.

Garvey asks, How does one get from our practical, little efforts to becoming all flame? His answer is that we continue to participate in the sacramental life of the church; we continue to seek God in prayer, fasting, silence, the scriptures, and sacraments. I would only add: We get there slowly.

We wait for the Lord. We repent and believe, day by day. Even when it seems as though little is happening.

Along the way, we will at times be who I was in that Texas retreat center, sitting in front of kindling, unable to start a fire, waiting.

Abba Lot can't force fire through his effort. And neither can I. Yet, in God's timing and by God's grace, all our little practices of perseverance, our faithful and flailing habits of prayer and work, of doubt and faith, of silence and listening, become the kindling that the Spirit of God mysteriously sets ablaze.

This is why we do not give up when we have grown weary. Not because we are promised that life will get easier, or because we must simply gut it out to the end, fearfully grasping a dying faith, but because, in due season, the harvest will come. We will be consumed by the presence of God. We become all flame.

I am, for now, still in the middle of my story. I have not yet stumbled on some oasis that makes my work, my faith, my relationships, and my days all seem fruitful, joyful, and vibrant. But I have witnessed what grows in weary lands. I have learned some things my cell is teaching me. I have hope that what has dwindled can spark to life and that what seems dead can be made new. I have found that, in the end, nothing will be wasted.

ACKNOWLEDGMENTS

This book has been a slow work, with many guides and helpers.

Thank you to my agent David McCormick for all his effort and encouragement, which made this project possible. Thank you to the whole Convergent team, especially Derek Reed, who showed patience, passion, and perseverance throughout the editing process.

Thank you to Marcia Bosscher, to whom this book is dedicated, for (as always) being my second reader and offering insight, advice, enthusiasm, and a listening ear.

Thank you to Shane and Kate Blackshear, David and Betsy Bixby, and Matthew Aughtry and Truett Seminary for generously providing space for me to write.

There are too many kind friends to thank. But to name just a few, thank you to my secret writing prayer team, who carried me. Thank you to fellow writers, especially those involved in the "intervention." Thanks to Blake Matthews and Krista Vossler and Walter and Morgan Stokes for encouraging me and praying for this book.

Thank you also to Kim Ramakrishnan and Rachel Welch for adopting one of my children each Tuesday so that I could write.

Profound thanks to George Hu for his vital support of my work.

Also thanks to everyone at Laity Lodge and LLFC for providing a gorgeous space for retreat and a place to hash out these inchoate ideas.

Thank you to Jon and Valerie Guerra for being sounding boards and cheerleaders, for the epic "title tea," for allowing me to use your space to work, and for your unfailing support for this project, from beginning to end. Thank you also to Joe Gleason for offering space to retreat and many prayers.

Thank you to Josh Jeter for invaluable feedback on this manuscript, for a shot in the arm when I most needed one, and for his abundant generosity and help.

Thank you to Woody Giles for editing help (and help in all of life).

Thank you to Immanuel Anglican church, which was born as I wrote this book. Friends there have offered prayer, encouragement, sympathy, love, and meals. Thank you also to Fr. Kester Smith for reading portions of this work.

Huge thanks to Carley Reigle, my colleague and director of operations, for her constant prayers, support, and help these past five years and throughout writing this book. It would not exist without her.

My deepest thanks to my children, Raine, Flannery, and Gus, who prayed for and rooted for this book. And were my happiest distractions from it. The time given to this work represents sacrifice on their part, and for that, I am grateful. Kids, you are deeply and always loved.

There is a story in the Bible where Moses must hold up his

arms to win a battle, but he gets exhausted and can't keep at it, so others hold them up. In this writing process, and over these years, Jonathan, my husband, has held up my arms in a thousand ways. Thank you for your help with research, your keen observations and edits, and your undying loyalty and love. There could not be enough thank-yous.

And glory be to the only one who makes beauty from ashes, to the Word, from whom any goodness in our little words flows, and by whom they will be redeemed.

NOTES

Epigraphs

1. Pierre Teilhard de Chardin, *The Making of a Mind: Letters from a Priest-Soldier 1914–1919* (New York: Harper & Row, 1961), 57–58.
2. Eugene H. Peterson, *A Long Obedience in the Same Direction: Discipleship in an Instant Society* (Downers Grove, Ill.: InterVarsity, 2019), 10.

1 | Discovery in the Desert

1. Galatians 6:9 (NIV).
2. In his journal, John Wesley famously described his initial conversion as an experience of having his heart "strangely warmed" while listening to Martin Luther's preface to the book of Romans being read aloud. John Wesley, *The Journal of John Wesley*, ed. Percy Livingstone Parker (Chicago: Moody, 1951), 55.
3. Claire Cain Miller, "Today's Parents: 'Exhausted, Burned Out and Perpetually Behind,'" *New York Times*, September 14, 2024, https://www.nytimes.com/2024/09/14/upshot/parents-stress

-murthy-warning.html; Louisa Kamps, "How to Care for Yourself as a Caregiver," *New York Times,* May 16, 2024, https://www.nytimes.com/2024/05/16/well/mind/caregiver-health.html; Charlie Warzel, "How to Leave an Internet That's Always in Crisis," *The Atlantic,* July 19, 2022, https://www.theatlantic.com/newsletters/archive/2022/07/quit-social-media-twitter-tiktok/676845/; Katie Mogg, "How Can I Avoid Burnout at Work?," *New York Times,* March 11, 2025, https://www.nytimes.com/2025/03/11/well/mind/work-burnout.html; Katie Glueck, "Anti-Trump Burnout: The Resistance Says It's Exhausted," *New York Times,* February 19, 2024, https://www.nytimes.com/2024/02/19/us/politics/trump-resistance-democrats-voters.html; Susan Krauss Whitbourne, "10 Signs of Burnout in a Relationship," *Psychology Today,* April 11, 2023, https://www.psychologytoday.com/us/blog/fulfillment-at-any-age/202304/10-ways-to-tell-if-your-relationship-suffers-from-burnout.

4. Ezra Klein, "Burned Out? Start Here," *New York Times,* January 7, 2025, https://www.nytimes.com/2025/01/07/opinion/ezra-klein-podcast-oliver-burkeman.html. Byung Chul Han's *The Burnout Society,* trans. Erik Butler (Stanford: Stanford University Press, 2015), made important early contributions to the conversation.

5. Adam Grant, "There's a Name for the Blah You're Feeling: It's Called Languishing," *New York Times,* April 19, 2021, https://www.nytimes.com/2021/04/19/well/mind/covid-mental-health-languishing.html; Adam Grant, "How to Stop Languishing and Start Finding Flow," TED, August 2021, https://www.ted.com/talks/adam_grant_how_to_stop_languishing_and_start_finding_flow. See also Corey Keyes, *Languishing: How to Feel Alive Again in a World that Wears Us Down* (New York: Crown, 2024).

6. Psalm 63:1 (ESV).

7. John of the Cross, *The Dark Night of the Soul,* in *The Complete Works of Saint John of the Cross, Doctor of the Church,* vol. 1, trans.

E. Allison Peers (Westminster, Md.: Newman, 1949), 315–457; Teresa of Ávila, "The Interior Castle," in *The Collected Works of Teresa of Avila,* vol. 2, trans. Kieran Kavanaugh and Otilio Rodriguez (Washington, D.C.: ICS Publications, 1980), 263–454.

8. Ignatius of Loyola, *The Spiritual Exercises of St. Ignatius,* trans. Louis J. Puhl (Westminster, Md.: Newman, 1951), 5.

9. Gisbertus Voetius and Johannes Hoornbeeck, *Spiritual Desertion,* trans. John Vriend and Harry Boonstra (Grand Rapids, Mich.: Baker Academic, 2003); William Ames, *The Substance of Christian Religion* (London, 1659), 128; Isaac Ambrose, *The Doctrine & Directions but More Especially the Practice and Behavior of a Man in the Act of the New Birth* (London, 1650), 46, 65.

10. Thomas Aquinas, *Summa Theologiae,* II.II q. 17 a. 3 ans., https://www.newadvent.org/summa/3017.htm.

11. Dom Benedict Hardy, "Work and Monasticism," *Humanum,* August 14, 2017, https://humanumreview.com/articles/work-and-monasticism.

12. John Chryssavgis, *In the Heart of the Desert: The Spirituality of the Desert Fathers and Mothers,* rev. ed. (Bloomington, Ind.: World Wisdom, 2008), 20.

13. Claudia Rapp, *Holy Bishops in Late Antiquity: The Nature of Christian Leadership in an Age of Transition* (Berkeley: University of California Press, 2005), 3–5, 143, 250.

14. Robert Doran, ed. and trans., *The Lives of Simeon Stylites* (Kalamazoo, Mich.: Cistercian Publications, 1992), 16.

15. Chryssavgis, *Heart of the Desert,* xii.

16. Richard Valantasis, *Centuries of Holiness: Ancient Spirituality Refracted for a Postmodern Age* (New York: Continuum, 2005), 178–80.

17. Chryssavgis, *Heart of the Desert,* 36.

18. Stanley M. Hauerwas, *Wilderness Wanderings: Probing Twentieth-Century Theology and Philosophy* (New York: Routledge, 1997), 25–31.

19. Chryssavgis, *Heart of the Desert,* 36.

2 | Stay in Your Cell

1. Jean-Charles Nault, *The Noonday Devil: Acedia, the Unnamed Evil of Our Times,* trans. Michael Miller (San Francisco: Ignatius, 2013), 23; Rowan Williams, *Silence and Honey Cakes: The Wisdom of the Desert* (Oxford: Lion, 2003), 83; Kathleen Norris, *Acedia & Me: Marriage, Monks, and a Writer's Life* (New York: Penguin, 2008), 20; Ken Parry, "The Nature and Scope of Patristics," in *The Wiley Blackwell Companion to Patristics,* ed. Ken Parry (Chichester, UK: John Wiley & Sons, 2015), 10.

2. Mariusz Finkielsztein, *The Sociology of Boredom* (Hoboken, N.J.: John Wiley & Sons, 2025), 178.

3. John Paul II, *Love and Responsibility,* trans. H. T. Willetts (San Francisco: Ignatius, 1983), 143.

4. Norris, *Acedia & Me,* 6.

5. Evagrius of Pontus, quoted in Gabriel Bunge, *Despondency: The Spiritual Teaching of Evagrius of Pontus,* trans. Anthony Gythiel (New York: SVS, 2012), 76; Benedicta Ward, trans., *The Desert Fathers: Sayings of the Early Christian Monks* (New York: Penguin Books, 2003), 66, 71, 79, 83, 92.

6. Arsenius, in Ward, *Desert Fathers,* 69.

7. "The stability that is here called for is not physical but spiritual. The whole mystery of the desert is encapsulated in this one concept of the cell." John Chryssavgis, *In the Heart of the Desert: The Spirituality of the Desert Fathers and Mothers,* rev. ed. (Bloomington, Ind.: World Wisdom, 2008), 42.

8. Benedict of Nursia, *The Rule of Saint Benedict Translated into English,* preface by W. K. Lowther Clarke (London: SPCK, 1931), chapters iv, lviii, lx, lxi, https://www.solesmes.com/sites/default/files/upload/pdf/rule_of_st_benedict.pdf.

9. Benedict, *Rule of Saint Benedict,* chap. lviii.

10. Hubert van Zeller, *The Holy Rule: Notes on St. Benedict's Legislation for Monks* (London: Sheed & Ward, 1958), 371.

11. Ward, *Desert Fathers,* 10.

12. Jen Pollock Michel, "A Habit Called Faith," Apprentice Gathering, 2022, https://www.youtube.com/watch?v=SyuNkR2yEOc. She adds in her book of the same title that even though "motions of faith" are not "faith itself . . . faith may have as much to do with habits as epiphanies." Michel, *A Habit Called Faith* (Grand Rapids, Mich.: Baker Books, 2021), 22.

13. Michel, "A Habit Called Faith."

14. Tish Harrison Warren, *Prayer in the Night: For Those Who Work or Watch or Weep* (Downers Grove, Ill.: InterVarsity, 2021), 8.

15. Mihaly Csikszentmihalyi, *Flow: The Psychology of Optimal Experience* (New York: Harper Perennial, 2008).

16. Anne Lamott (@ANNELAMOTT), "How to write: Butt in chair," X post, July 26, 2012, https://x.com/ANNELAMOTT/status/228366902668439552.

17. Philippians 4:9 (NIV).

18. 1 Timothy 4:15 (ESV). See also 1 Timothy 4:8.

19. This is a summary of the primary ideas in my first book, *Liturgy of the Ordinary* (Downers Grove, Ill.: InterVarsity Press, 2016).

20. Annie Dillard, *The Writing Life* (New York: Harper Perennial, 2013), 69.

21. Eugene H. Peterson, *A Long Obedience in the Same Direction* (Downers Grove, Ill.: InterVarsity, 2019), 188.

22. Macarius the Great, in Benedicta Ward, trans., *The Sayings of the Desert Fathers: The Alphabetical Collection,* Cistercian Studies Series 59 (Oxford: A. R. Mowbray, 1975), 111.

23. Peterson, *Long Obedience,* 188.

24. Athanasius, *The Life of Antony and the Letter to Marcellinus,* trans.

Robert Gregg, Classics of Western Spirituality (Mahwah, N.J.: Paulist, 1980), 39.

25. Gerald Brenan, *St. John of the Cross: His Life and Poetry* (Cambridge: Cambridge University Press, 1973), 26–28.

26. John of the Cross, *The Dark Night of the Soul,* in *The Complete Works of Saint John of the Cross, Doctor of the Church,* vol. 1, trans. E. Allison Peers (Westminster, Md.: Newman, 1949), 315–457; 330.

27. John of the Cross, *Dark Night,* 342.

28. John of the Cross, *Dark Night,* 367.

29. John of the Cross, *Dark Night,* 346.

30. John of the Cross, *Dark Night,* 351.

31. John of the Cross, *The Ascent of Mount Carmel,* in *The Complete Works of Saint John of the Cross, Doctor of the Church,* vol. 1, trans. E. Allison Peers (Westminster, Md.: Newman, 1949), 1–314; 13.

32. Psalm 131:2 (ASV).

33. Just to be clear, there are biblical commentaries that write on this idea in similar ways to how I do here, so this is not a novel insight. It is just that the people I happened to ask had not thought about this metaphor much. Others certainly have.

34. John of the Cross, *Dark Night,* 368.

35. John of the Cross, *Dark Night,* 368, 379.

36. Quoted in Williams, *Silence and Honey Cakes,* 87.

3 | Pledge Your Body to the Walls

1. Quoted in Rowan Williams, *Silence and Honey Cakes: The Wisdom of the Desert* (Oxford: Lion, 2003), 84.

2. Syncletica, in Benedicta Ward, trans., *The Sayings of the Desert Fathers: The Alphabetical Collection,* Cistercian Studies Series 59 (Oxford: A. R. Mowbray, 1975), 194.

3. Williams, *Silence and Honey Cakes,* 85.

4. Benedict of Nursia, *The Rule of Saint Benedict Translated into*

English, preface by W. K. Lowther Clarke (London: SPCK, 1931), chapter i.

5. John Wortley, trans., *More Sayings of the Desert Fathers* (Cambridge: Cambridge University Press, 2019), 134.

6. Sy Montgomery, *Of Time and Turtles: Mending the World, Shell by Shattered Shell* (New York: Mariner Books, 2023), 41.

7. Nicole Roccas, *Time and Despondency: Regaining the Present in Faith and Life* (Chesterton, Ind.: Ancient Faith Publishing, 2017), 67.

8. Kathleen Norris, *Acedia & Me: A Marriage, Monks, and a Writer's Life* (New York: Penguin, 2008), 1.

9. Roccas, *Time and Despondency,* 82.

10. Tish Harrison Warren, "As a Pandemic Parent, God Calls Me to This Loud and Lonely Life," *Christianity Today,* November 20, 2020, https://www.christianitytoday.com/2020/11/coronavirus-pandemic-parenting-motherhood-god-calls-life/.

11. Henri Nouwen, *The Genesee Diary: Report from a Trappist Monastery* (New York: Image, 1981), 71.

12. Ward, *Desert Fathers,* 60.

4 | Wait in the Womb

1. Taylor Swift, "I Can Do It with a Broken Heart," from *The Tortured Poets Department,* produced by Taylor Swift and Jack Antonoff, Republic Records, April 19, 2024.

2. Ryan Holiday, "You Know You're Good When . . . ," Daily Stoic, July 10, 2024, https://dailystoic.com/you-know-youre-good-when/.

3. A. A. Long, *From Epicurus to Epictetus: Studies in Hellenistic and Roman Philosophy* (Oxford: Clarendon, 2006), 256–57.

4. Quoted in Rowan Williams, *Silence and Honey Cakes: The Wisdom of the Desert* (Oxford: Lion, 2003), 97.

5. Daniel 3:25 (NIV).

6. C. S. Lewis, *The Collected Letters of C. S. Lewis,* vol. 3, *Narnia, Cambridge, and Joy, 1950–1963,* ed. Walter Hooper (New York: HarperCollins, 2004), 127.

7. John 16:33 (NKJV).

8. G. K. Chesterton, *Heretics* (New York: John Lane, 1919), 159.

9. Romans 5:3–4 (ESV).

10. Anthony C. Thiselton, *Discovering Romans: Content, Interpretation, Reception* (Grand Rapids, Mich.: Eerdmans, 2016), 126.

11. Douglas Moo, *Romans: The NIV Application Commentary* (Grand Rapids, Mich.: Zondervan, 2009), 171.

12. Chesterton, *Heretics,* 159.

13. Galatians 6:2.

14. Tish Harrison Warren, "What if Burnout Is Less About Work and More About Isolation?," *New York Times,* October 9, 2022, https://www.nytimes.com/2022/10/09/opinion/burnout-friends-isolation.html.

15. Pseudo-Athanasius, *The Life and Regimen of the Blessed and Holy Syncletica,* vol. 1, trans. Elizabeth Bryson Bongie (Eugene, Ore.: Wipf and Stock, 2003), 56.

16. Pseudo-Athanasius, *Life and Regimen,* 56.

17. C. S. Lewis, "The Weight of Glory," in *The Weight of Glory and Other Addresses* (New York: Macmillan, 1949), 4.

5 | Relax the Bow

1. Psalm 46:10 (ASV).

2. For example, in the New American Standard Bible (NASB)®. Copyright © 1960, 1971, 1977, 1995, 2020 by The Lockman Foundation. All rights reserved.

3. Poemen, in Benedicta Ward, trans., *The Desert Fathers: Sayings of the Early Christian Monks* (New York: Penguin Books, 2003), 5.

4. Rowan Williams, *Silence and Honey Cakes: The Wisdom of the Desert* (Oxford: Lion, 2003), 102, 104, 161.

5. Antony, in Ward, *Desert Fathers,* 88.
6. Poemen, in Ward, *Desert Fathers,* xvi.
7. Mary Karr, "As #writing gets harder, go at it softer," Facebook, October 23, 2023, https://www.facebook.com/MaryKarrLit/posts/pfbid02FSs3uuLzoEdPDz1XueXy85ZD3igi6XrFHHfB141ckfoHvfciiJok5jgTR1eg1j1l1.
8. Matthew 25:14–30.
9. Martin Shaw, "Staying Awake," The House of Beasts & Vines, January 21, 2024, https://martinshaw.substack.com/p/christianity-has-forgotten-its-a.
10. Thomas Merton, trans., *The Wisdom of the Desert: Sayings from the Desert Fathers of the Fourth Century* (London: Hollis and Carter, 1961), 34.
11. Quoted in Williams, *Silence and Honey Cakes,* 88.
12. Dorothy Day, *The Duty of Delight: The Diaries of Dorothy Day,* abridged edition, ed. Robert Ellsberg (New York: Image, 2011), 318.

6 | Let the Silt Settle

1. Benedicta Ward, trans., *The Desert Fathers: Sayings of the Early Christian Monks* (New York: Penguin Books, 2003), 11.
2. Portions of this story appeared in Tish Harrison Warren, "Want to Change the World? First, Be Still," *New York Times,* October 3, 2021, https://www.nytimes.com/2021/10/03/opinion/prayer-silence-activism.html.
3. Ward, trans., *Desert Fathers,* viii; Douglas Burton-Christie, *The Word in the Desert: Scripture and the Quest for Holiness in Early Christian Monasticism* (New York: Oxford University Press, 1993), 40–41, 54–56.
4. Josef Pieper, *Leisure: The Basis of Culture,* trans. Alexander Dru (New York: Pantheon Books, 1964), 4, 11.
5. Gregory the Great, *Morals on the Book of Job,* vol. 3, part 2 (Oxford: John Henry Parker, 1850), 366.

6. Blaise Pascal, *Pensées,* trans. A. J. Krailsheimer (New York: Penguin, 1966), 67.

7. Jonathan Bennett, "Glossary," in *Pensées* by Blaise Pascal, Some Texts from Early Modern Philosophy, https://www.earlymoderntexts.com/assets/pdfs/pascal1660.pdf.

8. "In contemporary society," writes the theologian Richard Foster, the devil "majors in three things: noise, hurry, and crowds." His suggestion for moving beyond "the superficialities of our culture, including our religious culture" is to embrace "the recreating silences . . . the inner world of contemplation." Richard Foster, *The Celebration of Discipline,* rev. ed. (San Francisco: Harper San Francisco, 1988), 15.

9. Pascal, *Pensées,* 69.

10. John Cassian, *How to Focus: A Monastic Guide for an Age of Distraction,* trans. Jamie Kreiner (Princeton: Princeton University Press, 2024), 131, 133. The monks also talk about the critical importance of discernment, the sifting of thoughts to determine their origin and trustworthiness, which Jamie Kreiner calls "detective work": "Some thoughts originated in the self. But God could also send thoughts into a monk's mind. So could demons. This meant that one's seemingly random thoughts were not all equally problematic. Some were good and some were bad. It was the job of the monk to tell the difference." Jamie Kreiner, *The Wandering Mind: What Medieval Monks Tell Us About Distraction* (New York: Liveright, 2023), 167.

11. Nicholas Carr, *The Shallows: What the Internet Is Doing to Our Brains* (New York: W. W. Norton, 2010).

12. Daniel Silver, "Boredom: An Introduction," *The Point,* no. 3, January 24, 2012, https://thepointmag.com/examined-life/boredom/.

13. Diadochus of Photiki, "On Spiritual Knowledge and Dis-

crimination," in G. E. H. Palmer et al., trans., *The Philokalia: The Complete Text,* vol. 1 (Boston: Faber & Faber, 1979), 276.
14. Andrew Sullivan, "I Used to Be a Human Being," *New York,* September 19, 2016, https://nymag.com/intelligencer/2016/09/andrew-sullivan-my-distraction-sickness-and-yours.html.
15. Syncletica, in Benedicta Ward, trans., *The Sayings of the Desert Fathers: The Alphabetical Collection,* Cistercian Studies Series 59 (London: A. R. Mowbray, 1975), 196.

7 | Brace the Wall

1. Jeremy Begbie, "Encountering the Uncontainable in the Arts," *God and Wonder: Theology, Imagination, and the Arts,* ed. Jeffrey W. Barbeau and Emily Hunter McGowin (Eugene, Ore.: Wipf and Stock, 2022), 114.
2. Gerard Manley Hopkins, "The Blessed Virgin Compared to the Air We Breathe," *Selected Poems of Gerard Manley Hopkins,* ed. Bob Blaisdell (Mineola, N.Y.: Dover Publications, 2011), 49. See also Edward T. Oakes, S.J., *Infinity Dwindled to Infancy: A Catholic and Evangelical Christology* (Grand Rapids, Mich.: Eerdmans, 2011).
3. Obadiah Sedgwick, *The Doubting Beleever* (London, 1653), 17.
4. Mark 9:24 (ESV).
5. John of the Cross, *The Dark Night of the Soul,* in *The Complete Works of Saint John of the Cross, Doctor of the Church,* vol. 1, trans. E. Allison Peers (Westminster, Md.: Newman, 1949), 395.
6. Psalm 44:9–19 (NIV).
7. Psalm 44:26 (NIV).
8. Walter Brueggemann, *The Message of the Psalms: A Theological Commentary* (Minneapolis: Augsburg Publishing House, 1984), 21.
9. Romans 8:35–36 (NIV). See also Psalm 44:22.
10. Romans 8:38–39 (NIV).
11. Andy Crouch, "Why Should You Doubt Your Doubts?," The

Veritas Forum (@veritasforum), Instagram reel, January 23, 2024, https://www.instagram.com/reel/C2ctXE3P3HF/.

12. John Cassian, *Conferences* 23.5 and 24.1, from C. S. Gibson, trans., *Nicene and Post-Nicene Fathers, Second Series,* vol. 11, ed. Philip Schaff and Henry Wace (Buffalo, N.Y.: Christian Literature Publishing, 1894). Accessed via New Advent, ed. by Kevin Knight, https://www.newadvent.org/fathers/350823.htm; https://www.newadvent.org/fathers/350824.htm.

13. John Wortley, trans., *More Sayings of the Desert Fathers* (Cambridge: Cambridge University Press, 2019), 105.

14. N. T. Wright, "Baptism: What Happens? Should We Baptise Infants?," *Ask NT Wright Anything* 107, March 3, 2022, https://opentheo.org/i/4503599627370518712/107-baptism-what-happens-should-we-baptise-infants.

15. See Gabriel Bunge, *Spiritual Fatherhood: Evagrius Ponticus on the Role of the Spiritual Father,* trans. Luis Joshua Salés (Yonkers, N.Y.: SVS, 2016), 38–40; Kenneth Leech, *Soul Friend: The Practice of Christian Spirituality* (San Francisco: Harper & Row, 1977), 41–49, 140–41.

16. Kevin J. Hart, "Poetry and Revelation: What It Means to Be a Christian Artist," ABC (Australian Broadcasting Corporation), February 17, 2021, https://www.abc.net.au/religion/kevin-hart-poetry-christianity-and-revelation/13165598.

17. Thérèse of Lisieux, *Story of a Soul: The Autobiography of Saint Thérèse of Lisieux,* 3rd ed., trans. John Clarke (Washington, D.C.: ICS Publications, 1996), 211–12.

18. Quoted in Richard Rohr, "Thérèse of Lisieux, Part V: Surrender to Love," Center for Action and Contemplation, August 7, 2015, https://cac.org/daily-meditations/therese-lisieux-part-v-surrender-love-2015-08-07/.

19. Thérèse, *Story of a Soul,* 213.

20. Thérèse, *Story of a Soul,* 257.

21. Quoted in Rohr, "Thérèse of Lisieux."
22. Tomáš Halík, *Patience with God: The Story of Zacchaeus Continuing in Us* (New York: Doubleday, 2009), 42.

8 | All Smoke, All Flame

1. Quoted in Charles Fountain, *Under the March Sun: The Story of Spring Training* (New York: Oxford University Press, 2009), 149.
2. Ezra Klein, "Burned Out? Start Here," *New York Times,* January 7, 2025, https://www.nytimes.com/2025/01/07/opinion/ezra-klein-podcast-oliver-burkeman.html.
3. Benedict of Nursia, *The Rule of Saint Benedict Translated into English,* preface by W. K. Lowther Clarke (London: SPCK, 1931), chapter iv.
4. Peter Leithart, *Solomon among the Postmoderns* (Grand Rapids, Mich.: Brazos, 2008), 69–70.
5. Ecclesiastes 12:13 (NIV).
6. Debra Rienstra, *Refugia Faith: Seeking Hidden Shelters, Ordinary Wonders, and the Healing of the Earth* (Minneapolis: Fortress, 2022), 1.
7. Joseph of Panephysis, in Benedicta Ward, trans., *The Sayings of the Desert Fathers: The Alphabetical Collection,* Cistercian Studies Series 59 (Oxford: A. R. Mowbray, 1975), 88.
8. John Garvey, "'Become All Fire': The Splendor of Orthodox Spirituality," *Commonweal,* February 25, 2008, https://www.commonwealmagazine.org/%E2%80%98become-all-fire.

ABOUT THE AUTHOR

Tish Harrison Warren is a writer and an Anglican priest. She is the author of several books, including *Liturgy of the Ordinary,* which was named *Christianity Today*'s Book of the Year, and *Prayer in the Night,* which won *Christianity Today*'s Book of the Year and the ECPA Christian Book of the Year. She formerly wrote a weekly newsletter for *The New York Times* that focused on faith in public discourse and private life. She was also a columnist at *Christianity Today.* Her articles and essays have appeared in *Comment, The Point,* and elsewhere. She currently serves as the C. S. Lewis Theological Writer-in-Residence for the Anglican Episcopal House of Studies at Baylor's George W. Truett Theological Seminary. She is a senior fellow with the Trinity Forum and an assisting priest at Immanuel Anglican Church. She lives in Austin, Texas, with her husband and three children.

tishharrisonwarren.com
Facebook.com/TishHarrisonWarrenAuthor
X: @Tish_H_Warren
Instagram: @tishharrisonwarren

ABOUT THE TYPE

This book was set in Baskerville, a typeface designed by John Baskerville (1706–75), an amateur printer and typefounder, and cut for him by John Handy in 1750. The type became popular again when the Lanston Monotype Corporation of London revived the classic roman face in 1923. The Mergenthaler Linotype Company in England and the United States cut a version of Baskerville in 1931, making it one of the most widely used typefaces today.